SEASONS OF COMMUNION

A Planning Workbook
For Sharing the Lord's Table
Through the Christian Year

Paul L. Escamilla

DISCIPLESHIP RESOURCES
MATERIALS FOR GROWTH IN CHRISTIAN FAITH & LIFE
—— NASHVILLE, TENNESSEE ——

❖ **TO PLACE AN ORDER** OR TO INQUIRE ABOUT RESOURCES AND CUSTOMER ACCOUNTS, CONTACT:

DISCIPLESHIP RESOURCES DISTRIBUTION CENTER
P.O. BOX 6996
ALPHARETTA, GEORGIA 30239-6996

TEL: (800) 685-4370

FAX: (404) 442-5114

❖   ❖   ❖

❖ **FOR EDITORIAL INQUIRIES** AND RIGHTS AND PERMISSIONS REQUESTS, CONTACT:

DISCIPLESHIP RESOURCES EDITORIAL OFFICES
P.O. BOX 840
NASHVILLE, TENNESSEE 37202-0840

TEL: (615) 340-7068

Cover and chapter opening designs by Tim Hornbeak.

Library of Congress Catalog Card No. 93-73816

ISBN 0-88177-130-9

DR130

 CONTENTS

❧ ACKNOWLEDGMENTS ❧

My thanks go to three congregations and several individuals for assistance in this work. First the congregations: St. Luke's United Methodist Church, Dallas, Texas, where these ideas were first germinated and shared; First United Methodist Church, Heath, Texas, where the Lord's Table was always spread with gladness, and where the substance of this work was completed; and Munger Place United Methodist Church, Dallas, my newest companion in ministry and worship, where this book has received its final borders.

As for individuals, my friend and colleague John Thornburg has been all along a resourceful, supportive reader; Craig Gallaway, Editorial Director at Discipleship Resources, has heightened my sense of the writing task with keen sensitivity and ability, as well as great generosity of time. The reviews of Hoyt L. Hickman, former Director of Resource Development in the Worship Unit at the General Board of Discipleship, have been helpful along the way, as has the delightfully soulful enthusiasm of his successor in that position, Dan Benedict. I appreciate Barbara Bate's addition to the work, Appendix B, pages 84-87.

At Bridwell Library I have received much support and courtesy from Page Thomas, Laura Randall, and the rest of the Bridwell staff.

I dedicate this book to my teacher, Don Saliers, in whose company I first came to delight in the Lord's Table and the Christian year; and to my wife Elizabeth, whose love for worship continues to deepen my own.

PART 1
STUDY

Introduction

Whoever can give their people better stories than the ones they have is like the priest in whose hands common bread and wine become capable of feeding the very soul.

HUGH KENNER[1]

How would you describe what the Lord's Supper means when it is shared in your church? Is it more an act of quiet reflection or of open celebration? Of introspection or outward focus? Of remembering or looking forward? Are there times when Holy Communion includes a mixture of all of these? Does the mixture vary from one season of the year to another?

When you leave worship on communion Sundays, do you sense that you have been nourished by the sacrament? What makes the Lord's Supper rich and meaningful for you over months and years of time?

In my work as a United Methodist pastor, and earlier as a layperson, these have been some of my questions and urgings about the ritual meal we call Holy Communion. If they are some of your questions as well — whether you are a worship leader or a participant, clergy or layperson — then I invite you to explore them more deeply within these pages.

WHERE WE ARE HEADING

The objective of this workbook is twofold: 1) To introduce the subjects of the Lord's Table and the Christian year, and 2) To develop understanding and confidence for planning and evaluating sacramental worship in your congregation through the seasons of the Christian year.

This is a book of study and reflection; it is also a book of planning and evaluation. It is intended to be carried from reading room to discussion group to sanctuary, and back again. It will call forth imagination, memory, and vision; it will also invite the use of Bibles, hymnals, and all the other tools of worship planning. It is for the person or group curious about what we call "the Lord's Supper" and "the Christian year" as well as the pastor or worship committee wanting to roll up sleeves and plan services of worship. *Seasons of Communion* is not a book just for "experts"; it is written as a friendly resource for all who love worship and who wish to see it deepened in their congregational setting. It is intended to make for good reading as well as good planning.

WORKBOOK FORMAT

The format of this workbook is sequential and is designed for ease of use. Part 1 presents a survey of the seasons of the Christian year and of certain meanings of Holy Communion within these seasons. This part is complete in itself and may be used by a "Discussion Group" with no planning responsibilities. A Sunday school class, for instance, would find in Part 1 seven self-contained study lessons on the Christian year, complete with discussion questions. If your group wishes to use Part 1 in this way, consider the following study schedule:

- First Session *(1 hour)*: Leader introduces the subject, using Chapter 1, "Introducing the Lord's Table and the Christian Year."

- Five Subsequent Sessions *(1 hour each)*: The group studies and discusses the five survey chapters on Advent, Christmas and Epiphany, Lent, Easter, and After Pentecost.

Part 1 also makes good reading for a pastor, music director, worship chairperson, or others who would benefit from a basic introduction to the Lord's Supper and the seasons of the Christian year.

Part 2 provides a complete set of exercises for a "Planning Group" wishing to translate its learnings from Part 1 into actual plans for congregational worship through the year. This kind of group can plan and prepare for each season of the Christian year by combining the planning activities of Part 2 with the study chapters of Part 1, weaving the two together as follows:

- Advent study followed by Advent planning
- Christmas and Epiphany study followed by Christmas and Epiphany planning
- Lent study followed by Lent planning
- Easter and Pentecost study followed by Easter and Pentecost planning
- After Pentecost study followed by After Pentecost planning

PLANNING GROUP MAKE-UP

If your group wishes to be involved in planning as well as study, then you will need to work with the pastor as well as with other worship leaders. The make-up of your group can take one of several forms, depending on the make-up of worship leadership in your congregation. Which of the following group structures (or some other) would make the most sense in your congregation?

- Worship committee with pastor, music director, and Christian educator
- Pastor, music director, Christian educator with selected persons, such as lay leader, worship committee chair, or other interested persons
- An open forum led by pastor, music director, and Christian educator

PLANNING GROUP SETTINGS AND SCHEDULES

The setting for these exercises of reading, sharing, and planning may be a retreat, a weekend workshop, a series of evening sessions, or even a Sunday school classroom. The book is structured in such a way that a group can choose to work through the study and planning sequence of one specific season without having to move directly into the materials for the next season. For example, an early October session might deal with Advent materials only (including the survey chapter on Advent, Chapter 2, and the regular planning chapters — 8 and 9). Later, a winter study could consider Lent (Chapter 4, with 8 and 9) or Easter and Pentecost (Chapter 5, with 8 and 9). A set of sessions in mid-summer could deal with any single set of chapters, the entire workbook, or, more briefly, the General Local Church Assessment (Chapter 7), which is appropriate for any time of the year.

The Introduction to Part 2 describes in more detail the specific functions of a Planning Group, and Appendix A offers several alternative schedules for such a group.

AS YOU BEGIN

It is my hope that, as you work through these chapters — whether you focus on study alone or proceed to planning — you will find out more about the ritual we call Holy Communion, gain some insights about your own thoughts and feelings toward the sacrament, and begin to come to worship on communion Sundays with a new sense of understanding and anticipation. For those who plan — clergy, diaconal ministers, lay planners — you are called to provide a faithful setting for the worship of God throughout the seasons of the year. When we are faithful to such work, and the Spirit blesses our efforts, then we may be assured that in our worship God will be glorified, and the bread and wine we share at the Lord's Table will indeed "become capable of feeding the very soul."

1. INTRODUCING THE LORD'S TABLE AND THE CHRISTIAN YEAR

Through the Eucharist, history becomes present and hope becomes reality. The past and future become actual here before our eyes. . . . The Church's year is indeed a year of grace.

PIUS PARSCH[1]

So teach us to count our days that we may gain a wise heart.

PSALM 90:12

THE CHRISTIAN YEAR

"Once upon a time . . ." marks the beginning of some of the very best fairytales. It also describes the way real life is lived; that is, "upon a time." Every experience, every action taken (or not), every encounter between persons happens in the context of time as we know it and as we live within it. The same is true of our encounters with God. When we place any of these experiences within a framework that can be recalled and understood, they become part of our way of "keeping time."

The Christian year is the church's way of keeping time, of remembering the history of our experiences with God. This "year" consists of seasons and special days observed on an annual calendar (see *The United Methodist Book of Worship*, p. 224). The calendar reflects two major cycles of events: 1. Advent, Christmas, Epiphany and 2. Lent, Easter, Pentecost.

Before, between, and following these two cycles are periods known as *ordinary time*. Thus, the calendar as a whole exhibits the following shape and flow:

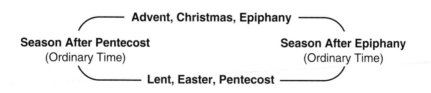

Advent, Christmas, Epiphany

Season After Pentecost
(Ordinary Time)

Season After Epiphany
(Ordinary Time)

Lent, Easter, Pentecost

How did the Christian calendar develop? A primary source was the biblical narrative. The Bible tells of God's actions in history and God's dealings with creation in ways that are reflected in the seasons of the year:

- **Advent:** The longings of creation and God's promise to save
- **Christmas and Epiphany:** The coming of God in Christ to save
- **Lent:** The call of discipleship and the divine suffering in the cross of Christ
- **Easter:** The triumph of God's grace in the resurrection of Jesus Christ
- **Pentecost:** The empowerment of God's people by the Holy Spirit for living and sharing the good news

The Christian calendar draws upon the language of time to tell and retell the biblical story of God's grace-filled, saving work in creation.

Beyond scripture, however, lies another source for the calendar's form and shape, having to do with our own life experience; for the cycles of the Christian year also reflect our own life cycles and experiences, and those of creation. Listen for the familiar: hunger and satisfaction; sowing and harvest; light emerging from darkness; guilt overcome by forgiveness; hope turned to joy; life, death, and new life. To live through the calendar year close to the cycles of the church year is to have our own story told and retold in the sacred language of seeking and finding, waiting and receiving, hungering and feasting, dying and being raised up.

Whether understood from the perspective of "the world of scripture" or from "the world of our lives," the Christian year expresses the tender care and provision of God for us and for all creation. From Advent hope through Christmas joy, Lenten suffering through Easter triumph, we experience in powerful ways the good news of God's love in Jesus Christ as it touches our own lives. We might say that the Christian year is the transforming embrace of our own stories by the Gospel story, as God patiently works to bring to fulfillment the work of love and justice begun and continued in and through us and all creation. The Christian year is, first, last, and all along the way, a year of grace.

THE LORD'S TABLE

If we could describe a meal that nourishes every part of our lives, what kind of meal would it be? Surely it would be a meal of thanksgiving and celebration, as well as one of commitment and self-surrender. The table for this meal would certainly be a place of encouragement through loneliness or hardship, and of healing in times of brokenness. It would be a place of empowerment and rejoicing, of enjoying the presence and company of those around it and of the one who spread the feast.

Such a table would be able to fill us up to satisfaction; to feed our hunger and quench our thirst, not for the sake of eating and drinking alone, but also to strengthen and refresh us for leaving that table. It would be a table with plenty and to spare, so that its bread could be taken and shared at other, lonelier tables. And there would certainly always be an empty place at the table, a constant reminder of those who have been excluded from its fellowship and nourishment.

In the church, there exists such a table; we call it the Lord's Table, or Holy Communion. And at this table a holy meal is shared again and again, season after season, year in and year out, generation to generation, among all who gather in Christ's name. At the table of the Lord we are fed and nourished in seasons of fasting and feasting, waiting and celebrating, longing and rejoicing. We come to the table of the Lord to find bread for our journey as people of faith; we leave that table with bread for the hungry world:

> Pour out your Holy Spirit on us gathered here,
> and on these gifts of bread and wine.
> Make them be for us the body and blood of Christ,
> that we may be for the world the body of Christ,
> redeemed by his blood.[2]

THE LORD'S TABLE THROUGH THE CHRISTIAN YEAR

When we consider the Lord's Table in the context of the various seasons of the Christian year, we begin to see the broad range of meanings and emotions expressed in our celebrations. We may experience Holy Communion one way in the season of recalling the Last Supper (Lent, Holy Week), and another in the season of recalling the "first supper" with the risen Lord as described by Luke in the Emmaus encounter (Eastertide). In the one, the disciples are having to say a final farewell to their teacher and Lord (Luke 22:14-20); in the other, they are greeting the risen Christ for the very first time (Luke 24:1-35)! The first setting is laden with heaviness of heart, Jesus' words of self-giving, and the imminence of a trial and crucifixion. The second is filled with mystery and wonder, unbridled joy and incredulity, and faith reborn through the witness of the resurrection.

Then there is the church in Acts sharing the Holy Meal in the wake of the sweeping Pentecost event (Acts 2:43-47); the sacramental taking, blessing, breaking, and sharing of bread by Jesus before thousands of hungry people who had just heard him teach (John 6:1-14); the haste and anticipation of the first Passover, with which the Last Supper itself was closely associated (Exodus 12:1-13); and the glorious image of people coming from east and west, north and south, to "sit at table in the kingdom of God" (Luke 13:29).

The Lord's Table through the Christian year is a meal calling forth many different emotions and responses. It is in certain seasons more a table of preparation — a time for making ready with repentance and self-giving; in others, of celebration — an occasion of enjoying with the worshiping community the good fruits of new creation. At certain times, the Eucharist calls forth remembrance and memorializing; at others, anticipation and hope. Through the seasons of the year, Holy Communion is a ritual of forgiveness and of empowerment for life in Christ; it is a meal of intimate communion with God and the faithful, and of sharing the bread with strangers far and wide.

In the pages ahead we will explore in greater depth the wealth of themes and meanings inherent in the Lord's Supper throughout the seasons of the Christian year. We will consider how the observance of Holy Communion in your congregation may be deepened as the Lord's Table is spread through these seasons. And we will look at how our lives — and our common life together — may be enriched when we are nourished from that table over time, season after season, year in and year out, from generation to generation.

2. THE SEASON OF ADVENT

We wait for everything that is really worth having. . . . We even wait for God.

ANTHONY PADOVANO[1]

Your kingdom come. Your will be done, on earth. . . .

MATTHEW 6:10

THE SEASON OF ADVENT

Since the fourth century, Advent has been observed by the church as a season of preparation. Early on, the length of the season was calculated backward forty days from the Epiphany (January 6), the day celebrating the inauguration of Jesus' public ministry. Later, the season's point of reference shifted to Jesus' birth, and four weeks prior to Christmas replaced the forty days preceding Epiphany as the designated time frame for Advent.

Despite this historical shift, the origins of Advent as a forty-day season are important. As we shall find again with Lent, forty is a number drawn from biblical references in which those who sought God, or strength, or home, spent forty days (or years) in a journey of preparation or seeking. Can you call to mind some examples of the use of the number forty in the Bible? Even a brief survey of biblical stories and accounts gives a strong impression of the significance of the number forty for those who found themselves waiting on or preparing for God.[2]

Advent is just such a preparation period, what we might call a "waiting" season. But what is the preparation — the waiting — all about? The meaning of the word *advent* yields a clue. The word is derived from the Latin word for "coming," and the first words of Advent are "God is coming," "Prepare the way of the Lord!"[3]

The "coming" to which Advent refers includes more than the Nativity. To be sure, the waiting of Advent is about preparing to commemorate the mystery and wonder of the coming of God in human flesh, the historic event that we often call the Incarnation (literally, the "embodiment"). Yet Advent is also about anticipating the coming of God in Christ in the future, when God's reign is finally and completely fulfilled in justice and peace. What is more, Advent is about preparing ourselves for the coming of Christ in grace here and now, "between the times," as it were, to be revealed in our hearts and lives as the indwelling presence of God.

Our waiting as Christians during Advent has to do with the "coming" of God in all of these ways — past, future, and present; in the flesh, in sovereign goodness, and in grace. One Advent prayer from *The United Methodist Hymnal* expresses all of these dimensions of our waiting. See if you can identify them:

> Merciful God,
> you sent your messengers the prophets
>   to preach repentance and prepare the way for our salvation.
> Give us grace to heed their warnings and forsake our sins,
>   that we may celebrate aright the commemoration of the nativity,
>   and may await with joy
>   the coming in glory of Jesus Christ our Redeemer; . . .[4]

Notice the "forward-leaning" that characterizes all three aspects of waiting. Past, present, and future dimensions of Advent preparation all express an expectancy, a hopefulness, for the reign of God to be fully manifested among us.

Yet in the process of yearning and waiting for the coming of God, we are brought to a close look at ourselves, our church, and our world, and we are forced to admit our own resistance to what we yearn for most: *"We are not ready,"* we might say. *"Our hearts are not quieted. Our lives are not in order. Our world is not just. Things are not yet as they ought to be, and we are not ready for the coming of God."*

When my oldest child, Sarah, was four years old, she and her two-year-old brother, David, had a typical on-and-off friendship, interrupted at regular intervals by spats over one thing or another. One day as they sat together in the grocery cart, Sarah reached over and gave David a big hug. It was a rare gesture, and I couldn't resist the question: "Do you love your brother, Sarah?" "Not yet," she answered cautiously.

Such a sense of "not-yetness" could be said to define virtually all of life's relationships. On one level we resist God's coming and what that would mean for our lives; but on another, as sure as a child's embrace, we deeply yearn for it.

One important biblical expression for that dual sense of resistance and yearning is the metaphor of hunger and its satisfaction.[5] From the creation stories in Genesis, through the accounts of judges and kings, to the prophets, and throughout the New Testament, hunger and its satisfaction are basic images related to waiting and finding, yearning and yielding, being lost from God and being found by God.[6]

During Advent we are reminded that hunger is not only a pervasive biblical theme, it is the very air we breathe as well. While television, Muzak, and storefront displays all point to this season as a time of festivity, abundance, and perpetual cheer, we need not look far beyond these sources to see a different picture. In our hearts and lives, in the church and in the world, the spiritual, emotional, and physical hungers are persistent and pervasive: loneliness, estrangement, spiritual lostness; violence, famine, warfare, greed. The moments of satisfaction, joy, and shared excitement through the season are well tempered by the awareness of these unfulfilled hungers.

While the world yearns in hunger, the promise of the Incarnation is that "far as the curse is found," God's blessings shall flow.[7] For no sooner have we heard the first words of Advent about the coming of God, becoming keenly aware of both our deep yearning and our profound unreadiness for that advent, than we hear Mary's song of hope, offered in thanksgiving and delight over God's promise of a Savior. Mary's song is only the first in a collection of sacred hope-songs in Luke's early chapters, none of them sung glibly. On the contrary, these joyful verses emerge from an awareness of brokenness and need in the world, making them all the more poignant in their truth-telling:

> God has shown great strength, scattering the proud. . . . God has brought down the powerful, and lifted up the lowly; God has filled the hungry with good things, and sent the rich away empty (Mary's song, Luke 1:51-53, paraphrase).

> Blessed be the Lord God of Israel, who has looked favorably upon God's people and has redeemed them. God has raised up a mighty savior for us . . . (Zechariah's prophecy, Luke 1:68-69, paraphrase).

> Master, now you are dismissing your servant in peace . . . for my eyes have seen your salvation . . . (Simeon's song, Luke 2: 29-30).

What these songs announce to us is that even as we wait for the promise of God, salvation has already come near! In Advent we receive as an already-present reality the promise that God will come in grace to redeem the world. Despite our unreadiness, our unworthiness, our resistance, our sin, God's grace has already made a home in our midst.

THE SEASON OF ADVENT AT THE LORD'S TABLE

What does it mean then to spread the Lord's Table in the season of Advent, to set a holy meal which is an expression of God's gracious reign, and our readiness, despite all obstacles, to receive it here and now?

Sharing the holy meal during the season of expectancy and waiting is an expression of the church's hope for God's deliverance in a world still caught in bondage and decay. The associations of the Eucharist with the tradition of the Passover meal remind us of the night on which the Hebrew children, slaves in Egypt, ate their bread in haste, staff in hand and one foot at the door, ready for their moment of deliverance (Exodus 12).

The Hebrew people in Egypt were not the last to hold bread in their hands with eyes raised to the horizon in expectation. Every people, every generation has lived that same prayer for the freedom of the oppressed and the healing of the nations. When we celebrate the Lord's Supper in Advent, we too stand at hope's door, staff in hand, waiting for God's deliverance as promised in the gift of a Savior. One of our Advent hymns, "Toda la Tierra," puts it in these words:

> All earth is waiting to see the Promised One,
> and the open furrows, the sowing of the Lord.
> All the world, bound and struggling, seeks true liberty;
> it cries out for justice and searches for the truth.[8]

To hold in our hands the bread of the sacrament is to claim for ourselves and for the whole creation the deliverance promised by God. Therein lies the intention of the congregational acclamation, found at the heart of the eucharistic Prayer of Great Thanksgiving: "Christ has died; Christ is risen; Christ will come again." These words are as much a prayer as they are a proclamation, as much words of assurance as profession of faith, echoing the invocation found at the end of Revelation: "Come, Lord Jesus!"

Along with the yearning that is ingredient to Advent hope, there is another dimension of that hope that is much like preparation for a family dinner around the holidays. Anticipation swells with the eagerness to see family and share the joy of being united. Of course there is work to be done — a house to clean, a table to set, and a meal to prepare. But this is preparation we enjoy, for every task leads us closer to the glad feast with those we love. The festive Advent hymn, "People, Look East," conveys this sense of making ready, not in fear, but with great anticipation:

> People, look east. The time is near of the crowning of the year.
> Make your house fair as you are able, trim the hearth and set the table.
> People, look east: Love, the Guest, is on the way.[9]

Holy Communion in Advent is a sign of the kind of future we look for as a result of God's reign. It points to the day when earth's harvest of food will be fully shared, the hungry fed, the poor raised up, and the reign of God made wholly manifest. To gather for Holy Communion during the season of Advent is to taste and see the nearness of the reign of God which is "on the way," yet already manifested among us now in ways we can glimpse and enjoy in our table fellowship.

CONCLUSION

Frederick Robertson, the great English preacher of the last century, used to say that John the Baptist served up no fancy dishes, but with his bare hands broke the bread of God and said, "Eat this and live." Advent around the Lord's Table is a time of getting ready for the coming of God by identifying our own hungers and the hungers around us, and looking to the life-giving bread of God for satisfaction of those hungers. Having been nourished in our waiting, we are given the grace by which to share that nourishment with others through concrete acts of compassion and mercy. This is the bread of God for us, and to eat it is to be made truly alive.

❦ For Reflection and Discussion ❧

1. As a group, share experiences (from childhood or adulthood) of waiting for things material, intangible, welcome, and unwelcome. In what ways is "waiting for Christmas" in the popular sense similar to waiting for God's coming, and for new creation? In what ways are these different?

2. It has been said that before the gospel is ever heard as good news, it is first heard as bad news. Turn to Luke 1:46-56, the declaration known as "Mary's song." Divide into two groups, the delighted and the disgruntled. Give the two groups three minutes to study the text. Have the "disgruntled" group present the reasons they are displeased with the song, the "delighted" group, why they are pleased.

3. As a class or in small groups, create a paraphrase of "Mary's song," based on the group's gathered beliefs and understandings about what it would mean for God's reign to be fulfilled in the modern world. Write these words and descriptive phrases on newsprint or on a chalkboard.

4. Now discuss ways in which the congregation's (and individual families') life together during Advent can reflect more closely the vision the group has compiled.

5. Invite group members to imagine themselves in the original Passover (Exodus 12) — staff in hand, foot at the door — as they eat in haste the bread that will tide them over to freedom. Discuss ways in which the Lord's Supper can be understood as a meal of expectancy and anticipation, of getting ready for liberation. How is this similar to or different from normal understandings of this meal within your congregation?

6. Share the Lord's Supper, if this can be arranged.

Planning groups proceed to Chapter 8, "Assessment."

3. THE SEASON OF CHRISTMASTIDE AND AFTER EPIPHANY

In the juvescence of the year
Came Christ the tiger . . .

T.S. ELIOT[1]

And one called to another and said:
"Holy, holy, holy is the Lord of hosts:
the whole earth is full of his glory."

ISAIAH 6:3

THE SEASONS OF CHRISTMAS, EPIPHANY, AND AFTER EPIPHANY

If Advent has to do with preparing for a banquet, then the seasons of Christmas and the Epiphany are the feast itself. Advent has given voice to our hope in the promise of God to save us; Christmas and the Epiphany invite us to celebrate the fulfillment of that promise in the gift of Jesus Christ. One of the most beloved Christmas hymns announces this good news with great boldness and joy:

> Joy to the world, the Lord is come!
> Let earth receive her King;
> let every heart prepare him room,
> and heaven and nature sing . . .[2]

These are days of joy and singing, for us and for all creation; for the Lord has come! During these days we discover and celebrate the gift of God manifested in the birth of a child; we celebrate the very coming of God in the flesh.

"Incarnation" is what we call this act of God becoming flesh in Jesus the Christ, and Christmas, Epiphany, and the season following all serve to "flesh out" the material richness of this event. There is a newborn child in a manger, angel-struck shepherds smelling of sheep, costly aromatic gifts from traveling magi, flowing waters at the Jordan, good wine at a wedding, and name after name of ordinary-person-turned-follower-of-Jesus. This is incarnation: the extraordinary filling the ordinary; God's glory manifested in earthly things.

CHRISTMAS

It all begins with Christmas. The "Christ Mass" was originally a reference to the service of worship on December 25 commemorating the birth of Jesus (Luke 2:1-20). Now the season of Christmas, or Christmastide, refers to the period from December 25 (or December 24 when there is a Christmas Eve service) through January 6 during which the church celebrates the birth of Jesus and the coming of God in flesh. In essence, Christmastide is a twelve-day season, of which the song "The Twelve Days of Christmas" is a popular reminder.

THE EPIPHANY

The crown of the Christmas season is that thirteenth day — January 6, the day of Epiphany. *Epiphany* (literally, "to make very clear") is a word drawn right from scripture, from John's first account of Jesus' ministry (John 2:1-11). The setting is a wedding feast, and Jesus is there. The wine is flowing, and we can imagine music and dancing, laughter and singing. It is a festive day, and hearts are glad. Then, suddenly, the wine gives out. And, in what John describes as a "sign," Jesus turns water into wine — good wine and plenty of it! "Jesus did this, the first of his signs, in Cana of Galilee," John tells us, "and revealed ([epi]phanero) his glory . . ." (John 2:11).

Over the centuries, the observance of the Epiphany has focused on other "revelations" or "manifestations" of God's glory found early in the Gospel narratives. Specifically, the visit of the magi (Matthew 2:1-12) and the baptism of Jesus (Matthew 3:13ff and parallels) have been observed in different traditions on the day of Epiphany. In The United Methodist Church, and throughout what is often called the "Western church" (Roman Catholic and Protestant church traditions), Epiphany recalls the visit of the magi to the Christ child. In certain Spanish-speaking traditions, the day is named accordingly: "Dia de los Reyes," or "Three Kings Day."

As festive as the day of Epiphany is, it contains a tragic dimension as well. For no sooner has the news spread of the birth of a holy child than the sword of Rome is brought down upon the innocent (Matthew 2:16-18). The magi have traveled a course of spiritual pilgrimage, but in so doing they have left a trail upon which the deceitful and cruel will also travel. Martin Luther once observed that when God's people build a church, the devil builds a chapel. Even at Christmastime — perhaps especially so — the gospel meets with profound resistance.

THE SEASON AFTER THE EPIPHANY

During the season After the Epiphany, references to Jesus' early ministry and the showing forth of God in that ministry appear in the Gospel readings provided by the lectionary. This season is often referred to as "Ordinary Time," not in a diminutive way, but suggesting the ongoing path of discipleship we are called to follow — beyond the manger, the angels, the star, the magi, and the dove. Howard Thurman puts that call in these terms:

> When the song of the angels is stilled,
> When the star in the sky is gone,
> When the kings and princes are home,
> When the shepherds are back with their flock,
> The work of Christmas begins:
>> To find the lost,
>> To heal the broken,
>> To feed the hungry,
>> To release the prisoner,
>> To rebuild the nations,
>> To bring peace among brothers and sisters,
>> To make music in the heart.[3]

Having beheld God's glory, we could say we become "beholden" to it — that is, grasped by it, held by it, inwardly persuaded by it. In our response, we now become the vessels of God's glory revealed.

The Seasons of Christmas, Epiphany, and After Epiphany at the Lord's Table

Christmas Eve and Christmas Day

For the church to observe the arrival of Christmas with Holy Communion is a joyful recognition that, in the birth of Jesus, God has come among us in fullest measure! In the fullness of time God sent Jesus, born of a woman, as the Word become flesh, and mystery and wonder accompany every observance of that event. In Holy Communion, shared on this occasion, earthly things become signs of incarnation, as common bread and wine are transformed into the bread of heaven and the cup of salvation:

> As your Word became flesh, born of woman, on that night long ago,
> so, on the night in which he gave himself up for us, he took bread,
> gave thanks to you, broke the bread, gave it to his disciples, and said:
> "Take, eat; this is my body which is given for you."[4]

All earth has been in eager longing for the redemption of God. Now we gather at the table of the Lord, bringing with us the fruits of the earth, to celebrate the news that with Messiah's birth, earth's redemption has come. Bread and wine on this day are signs of the filling up of all creation with the life and splendor of God:

> Joy to the world, the Savior reigns!
> Let all their songs employ;
> while fields and floods, rocks, hills, and plains repeat the sounding joy . . .[5]

The Epiphany

The Epiphany of the Lord is celebrated in the church either on the day of Epiphany (January 6) or on the first Sunday in January. In either case, the occasion is, for most congregations, a communion Sunday. As we have already seen, the season of Christmastide is filled with symbols and signs which are both materially and spiritually rich: gifts of magi, wine at a feast, and others. Such imposing images all join in announcing that God's salvation has come tangibly and clearly, here and now; God's reign has become manifest in the present hour:

> Now the hearing   Now the power
> Now the vessel brimmed for pouring
> Now the body   Now the blood
> Now the joyful celebration
>
> Now the wedding   Now the songs
> Now the heart forgiven leaping
> Now the Spirit's visitation
> Now the Son's epiphany
> Now the Father's blessing
> Now   Now   Now[6]

This communion hymn is beautifully clear in its immediacy, leaving no time even for punctuation! The Epiphany feast is a proclamation that God is with us, and God is with us now! I remember the way one pastor brought this reality to words years ago during an Epiphany service. In the opening exchange of the great thanksgiving prayer, the presider normally says, "The Lord be with you," to which the people respond, "And also with you." This pastor's greeting, slightly altered, became a joyful declaration of the Epiphany: "The Lord is with you!" she announced. "And also with you!"

But we also know this about the Epiphany feast: Wheat is ground, and grapes are crushed to prepare for such a joyful meal as this. Bread is broken and wine poured out to make the feast. We are no strangers to the pain of the world; it is also our pain. And we know it does not cease simply because it is Christmas; for many, it is only more acute. The magi, beholding the glory of Christ, answered in joyful adoration; Herod answered in a different manner altogether, with the slaughter of the innocents. As a result, the story of Jesus' birth includes one of the two most violent events recorded in Matthew's Gospel, the other being the crucifixion.

We spread the Lord's Table during Christmas and the Epiphany in joy and singing, but fully aware that the power that moved Herod still works its destruction, and earth is yet to fully receive its Savior. Amid joy and thanksgiving, lamentation and weeping, the gift of this holy meal, which announces the coming of God in the world to heal and to save, is all the more to be savored.

The Season After the Epiphany

As mentioned earlier, the season After the Epiphany is known as Ordinary Time. In certain respects, however, there is nothing at all ordinary about this season! The Baptism of the Lord (the first Sunday after the Epiphany) presents a natural occasion for a service of congregational reaffirmation of the baptismal covenant (see p. 50 in *The United Methodist Hymnal*), which may include the Lord's Supper. Alternately, this Sunday may involve the congregation in a service of covenant renewal (see p. 288 in *The United Methodist Book of Worship*), if such has not been used on New Year's Eve or Day (also pp. 288-89 in the *Book of Worship*). Covenant renewal can also be observed at any other time through the season. Whenever this traditional Wesleyan service is used, it is an especially appropriate occasion for the celebration of the holy meal.

Spreading the Lord's Table during the season After the Epiphany is an invitation for the church to fill out the meaning of God-with-us for our life together as a congregation. John spoke of Jesus' miracle at Cana as "the first of his signs," leading us right away to anticipate that there will be more to follow. By now there has been a great fulfillment — we have seen and celebrated the good news of a Savior's birth, and the beginning of Jesus' ministry. And yet, even in the midst of these events, there is great anticipation of what is yet to follow.

Part of that anticipation has to do with how our own response to the Incarnation will be "fleshed out"; for the encounters of Christmas and Epiphany, after all, have moved in two directions — *from* God, to be sure; but also *to* God: Christ is born into the world, and gifts of magi are offered to the holy child; wine is given at the Cana wedding for all to enjoy, and a claim is made upon the lives of certain fishermen (Matthew 4:18ff and parallels).

The observance of the communion feast during the season after the Epiphany can be understood as a celebration of God's gift to us, as well as an offering, in response, of our finest gifts to God. Borrowing from T.S. Eliot, we can put that dynamic in the form of a question: When "Christ the tiger" comes into our lives in the newness of the year, what is likely to happen? To what response will such an epiphany, such a making-God's-glory-very-clear lead us? The first disciples beheld Christ's glory and responded with believing (John 2:11). And we? What will be our faith response?

> You satisfy the hungry heart with gift of finest wheat.
> Come, give to us, O saving Lord, the bread of life to eat.
> You give yourself to us, O Lord; then selfless let us be,
> to serve each other in your name in truth and charity.[7]

CONCLUSION

In the Christmas service, the service of the Epiphany, the service of congregational reaffirmation of Baptism, and the covenant renewal service, we experience the Lord's Table as a place of receiving the good news of a long-awaited Savior and of beholding the glory of God in Christ. We bring to the table our own gifts — whatever they are, to honor the one whose gift is God-with-us. Offerings of renewed commitment and service, devotion and talents, the gift of our very selves — these are our response to the transforming gift of God in Jesus the Christ. The power of that singular gift to work in and through our lives as we leave the glad feast is expressed with the words of this post-communion prayer:

> You have given yourself to us, Lord.
> Now we give ourselves for others.
> Your love has made us a new people:
> As a people of love we will serve you with joy.
> Your glory has filled our hearts;
> Help us to glorify you in all things.[8]

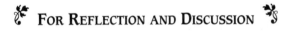

FOR REFLECTION AND DISCUSSION

1. Recall experiences of a great banquet or feast. What were the elements that made these so special?

2. Ask any in the class who may have seen the movie "Babette's Feast" to describe the meal that is the climax of that film.

3. Discuss ways in which the Lord's Supper could be understood as a joyful feast such as those that have been described. What sometimes prevents it from being so understood?

4. In the light of Matthew 2:16-18 (the massacre of the infants), recall situations in which a wonderful experience has been interrupted by tragedy. In what sense do Christmas and the season of Christmastide function to highlight tragic dimensions of life? Share some examples (e.g., visiting nursing homes, an increase in suicides, harsh weather for the homeless).

5. How should we respond in the face of such "interruptions" to the festivity of the season?

6. What are some ways the congregation can otherwise serve to "manifest the glory" of God in the world in the season around the Epiphany?

7. Share the Lord's Supper, if this can be arranged.

Planning groups proceed to Chapter 8, "Assessment."

4. THE SEASON OF LENT

This is the time of tension between dying and birth.

T.S. ELIOT[1]

For as often as you eat this bread and drink the cup, you proclaim the Lord's death until he comes.

1 CORINTHIANS 11:26

THE SEASON OF LENT

With the season of Lent we begin a new cycle in the Christian year, what we call the Lent, Easter, Pentecost cycle (see diagram, page 5). The season of Lent is a part of Easter in a similar way that Advent is a part of Christmas: The one is preparation for the other. The purpose of Lent, we could say, is to bring us to Easter appropriately.

The season of Lent originated as a period of forty days prior to Easter during which new converts were to prepare for Easter baptism with a period of fasting and devotion. We might be reminded by the length of the season of the roots of Advent, and of the many biblical images of preparation and waiting which involve forty days or years (see Chapter 2, note 2).

Ash Wednesday (forty days prior to Easter, excluding Sundays) marks the beginning of the season. The day is named for the service observed in many congregations in which ashes are imposed upon the forehead (see *The United Methodist Book of Worship*, pp. 321ff). The ashes serve as both a reminder of mortality and an invitation to repentance, setting the tone for the entire season of Lent. Hence the words which are a central feature of the service:

Remember that you are dust, and to dust you shall return.
Repent, and believe the gospel.[2]

The tone and intention of the season of Lent are further established through the lectionary Gospel reading for the first Sunday in Lent, always the narrative of Jesus' forty days in the wilderness (Matthew 4:1-11 and parallels). To enter Lent is to enter a season of repentance, humility, and learning what it means to surrender our lives to God's grace and sustenance.

Lent is a word derived from an Anglo-Saxon word for "spring"; yet with such beginnings to the season, we have to wonder what Lent could possibly have to do with the season of spring! Here we are situated in the desert, our foreheads marked with ashes, and we are to compare it to the budding, greening, and warming of the earth?

The answer to this seeming contradiction may be found in this dynamic reality: Through attention to the Spirit in the season of Lent, our lives are raised up from brokenness to wholeness, and from death to new life. For while the world lives in ongoing tension between birth and dying, the church moves through Lent within the tension between dying and new birth. The "desert season" teaches us that discipleship in Christ is not intended to equip us for easing from life toward a pleasant death, but to empower us for laying down our lives in order to move from death to new life. Remember the springtime-harvest image used by Jesus, ". . . unless a grain of wheat falls into the earth and dies . . ." (John 12:24*a*).

THE SEASON OF LENT AT THE LORD'S TABLE

Take, bless, break, and share. This is the four-fold action of the holy meal we call the Lord's Supper. We can identify this pattern in various New Testament accounts in which Jesus is sharing the provision of bread, including the feeding of the five thousand (Mark 6:41 and parallels), the Emmaus encounter on the day of resurrection (Luke 24:30), and the Last Supper: "Jesus took bread, and when he had given thanks he broke the bread, gave it to his disciples . . ." (Matthew 26:26). At one level, the action describes what is literally taking place with the bread in those settings; but at another, it is saying something about the one who holds the bread and offers it, as well as those who are to receive.

"This is my body, which is given for you," Jesus said during the Last Supper (Luke 22:19), as if to mean, "This is my body, taken, blessed, broken, and shared" with the world. His very life and ministry confirm this: Jesus' life has been taken and set apart by God, blessed for ministry, broken through suffering, and shared in self-giving.

In John's Gospel, the Passover meal is accompanied by Jesus' washing the disciples' feet, and the command, ". . . I have set you an example, that you also should do as I have done to you" (John 13:15). Hence, sharing the meal of Holy Communion is a sign of Christ's offering of himself to us (his life taken, blessed, broken and shared with the world) but also of God's people being offered for others, along the same pattern. Following Jesus in discipleship, our lives are continually being taken, blessed, broken, and shared; that is, claimed and set apart (taken), prepared and anointed by God (blessed), then surrendered in the service of the gospel (broken and shared).

One of our hymns from the Spanish-language tradition depicts beautifully the binding of God's self-giving with our own in the sacrament, drawing upon the realities of suffering and sacrifice as dimensions of faithful life in the world:

Sheaves of summer turned golden by the sun,
grapes in bunches cut down when ripe and red,
are converted into the bread and wine of God's love
in the body and blood of our dear Lord.

We are sharing the same communion meal,
we are wheat by the same great Sower sown;
like a millstone life grinds us down with sorrow and pain,
but God makes us new people bound by love.[3]

The ritual of the Lord's Supper expresses this connection as well. As we share the eucharistic meal, God's self-giving in Christ and our own self-giving in ministry are woven together. The conclusion of the prayers of Great Thanksgiving is only one instance where this association is made:

Pour out your Holy Spirit on us gathered here,
and on these gifts of bread and wine.
Make them be for us the body and blood of Christ,
that we may be for the world the body of Christ,
redeemed by his blood.[4]

See if you can identify other instances in which themes of taking, blessing, breaking, and sharing find expression in the communion liturgy. Where do these refer to God's self-giving? Where to our own? And to both?

Lent offers multiple occasions for observing the "take-bless-break-share" meal: Ash Wednesday, when we move from the ashes of mortality and repentance to receive the bread and wine of self-offering and surrender (*Book of Worship*, pp. 321ff); Lenten Sundays generally (*BOW*, pp. 60-63); Passion, Palm Sunday (*BOW*, p. 338); Maundy (or Holy) Thursday, the day on which the Last Supper and the washing of the disciples' feet are both commemorated (*BOW*, p. 351). The Services of Healing presented in *The Book of Worship* (pp. 613-26) are further opportunities for sacramental participation during the season. If a study or prayer group meets during Lent, or if there is a family night or early morning breakfast, the Eucharist can become an intrinsic part of such gatherings.

Conclusion

Observance of Holy Communion during Lent provides a pathway on the Lenten journey along which our congregations may draw nearer in devotion to the Christ whose life was taken, blessed, broken, and shared with the world. Further, in the fertile ground of springtime-Lent, nearness to the sacrament can become a means by which we experience our own lives taken up by God, consecrated for serving, and shared with the world. Springtime has its origins in the wilderness, and new life begins when we choose to surrender our lives to God in self-giving, a process in which healing and renewal accompany devotion and self-surrender:

Take our bread, we ask you;
take our hearts, we love you.
Take our lives, O Father, we are yours, we are yours.

• • •

Your holy people standing washed in your blood,
Spirit-filled yet hungry we await your food.
We are poor, but we've brought ourselves the best we could;
we are yours, we are yours.[5]

❦ FOR REFLECTION AND DISCUSSION ❧

1. Ask any in the group who have participated in a service of ashes or of footwashing to share their experience. What is suggested by such actions about the "dying" dimension of Christian life?

2. Discuss the paradox contained within the claim that we become truly alive through dying, that springtime begins in the desert. Can the group confirm the truth of this claim? Discuss the differences between self-denial and self-loathing.

3. Use a loaf of bread to move through the take-bless-break-share action. Ask the group to join you in these actions with their own gestures. Talk about ways in which the sacrament, by language, elements, movements, and other dimensions, draws worshipers into a posture of self-offering.

4. Now ask the group, with eyes closed, to imagine a piping hot loaf of bread just as it is being broken in the middle. What sensory impressions come to mind? (e.g., steam rising, warmth, aroma, energy released, mouth watering). With eyes still closed, lead the group through a guided experience in which their lives, placed in God's hands, are taken, blessed, broken, and shared.

5. Discuss ways in which we understand our lives beyond the sanctuary to be offered in this way to God and to others.

6. Share the Lord's Supper, if this can be arranged.

Study groups proceed to Chapter 8, "Assessment."

5. THE SEASON OF EASTERTIDE

. . . When Jesus took bread and wine or a few fish and blessed God for them and shared them with his disciples, creation found its purpose once again.

MARK SEARLE[1]

But in fact Christ has been raised from the dead, the first fruits of those who have died.

1 CORINTHIANS 15:20

THE SEASON OF EASTERTIDE

Stretching from the day of Jesus' resurrection to the day of Pentecost, the season of Eastertide has been referred to for centuries as the "Great Fifty Days," a period of celebration and witness, disbelief turning to joy (Luke 24:41), and broadcasting the incredible (Acts 2:1-40). For the early church, Easter was a season of far greater importance than its predecessor, Lent. The feasting that follows the resurrection is always understood to be greater than the fasting that precedes it.

Easter's tone of awe and great joy is reinforced again and again throughout fifty days of scripture narratives that tell of certain disciples overwhelmed at the sight of an empty tomb (Luke 12:1-12 and parallels), others hiding behind locked doors (John 20:1-12), breakfast on the seashore with the risen Christ (John 21:1-14), the promise of the Holy Spirit (Luke 24:44-49), and tongues loosed for witness (Acts 2:1-13). In the Gospel accounts as well as in the beginning pages of Acts, the report is that something profoundly life-giving is stirring in the shadow of the empty tomb.

And yet, the question must be asked, "What is Easter about outside the New Testament?" We know that the season commemorates Jesus' resurrection from the dead and the disciples' encounters with their risen Lord, but what does that mean for us, or for the world, today? What precisely do we celebrate as the church during "the great fifty days"?

At one level, Easter means a new order for our lives, and for the life of the church — a new order within our own lives, we could say, and within the

Christian community. After the resurrection, there is greater fear, greater joy, more gasping, and more running recorded in the Gospels than ever mentioned before that event. The disciples of Jesus are drastically affected by what they see and hear. Initially, these appear to be spontaneous, "gut-level" reactions to what has happened. Then, gradually, that external sign — Jesus' resurrection — becomes internalized, and deep change begins to happen within the band of Jesus' followers. "Reaction" turns to "response" as the beholders of resurrection become witnesses to it. By Pentecost, their awe and incredulity have found a voice:

> Lose your shyness, find your tongue;
> tell the world what God has done.
> God in Christ has come to stay.
> Live tomorrow's life today![2]

Shifting from the role of observers to that of participants — this is the experience of Easter, not only in scripture, but in our lives as well. The commemoration of the resurrection of Christ from the dead is not primarily about observing a relic of some kind — whether the image of an empty tomb, the Gospel story itself, or simply a sunny spring day designated on the calendar as Easter. Easter is about participating personally and as a community of faith in the very same reality that raised Jesus from the dead — the grace and power of God at work to transform lives, indeed all creation. Easter has to do with allowing the miracle of a risen Lord to become a sign of resurrection within us, a promise of our own lives raised up to wholeness and witness, through faith in the risen Christ. For "If the Spirit of him who raised Jesus from the dead dwells in you, he who raised Christ from the dead will give life to your mortal bodies also . . ." (Romans 8:11).

At another level, Easter means new life not only for the individual and for the church, but for the world as well. All the forces amassed in favor of death for this radical Galilean prophet named Jesus were utterly disarmed in the resurrection event, and a new order took their place. I recently viewed an exhibit of medieval art from the Russian Orthodox tradition in which one painting depicted the resurrection scene as Matthew describes it. The illustrious angel dominates the painting; the two women disciples stand at the side, seized with wonder; and, in a corner of the painting, almost as a footnote, two miniature Roman guards, looking like tiny toy soldiers, stiff and wooden, lie faint on the ground. Their swords, like toothpicks, rest on the ground beside them. In the wake of resurrection, the evil power that moved Rome and its partner, the religious hierarchy, to such oppression has been benevolently vanquished; its once formidable guardians have been turned to mere playthings.

The resurrection of Jesus from death means that the world now turns according to a new order — what we sometimes call the peaceable rule of God or the kingdom of God. In the old order, the rule of life and community was based upon domination and was reinforced by the sword; in the new, the rule has its basis in freedom and reconciliation, and angels atop rolled-away stones are giving the orders! This new reality was denied from the start by the religious leaders and local authorities (see Matthew 28:11ff), as it often is now. But the reality remains nonetheless: In the resurrection, the beginnings of a new creation have burst forth for all witnesses, welcoming or otherwise, to behold and to share.

Personally, for the Christian community, and for the world, the resurrection of Jesus from the dead shakes the foundations, and from the rubble emerge new life, new relationships, and a new order, all pointing back to that first-fruits event, and forward to the fulfillment of that event in the great and final harvest of new creation.

THE SEASON OF EASTERTIDE AT THE LORD'S TABLE

The bread of resurrection is found in abundance — and shared generously — in the Easter Gospels and the Easter church. Luke's Gospel tells of two forlorn disciples — perhaps husband and wife, or good friends — traveling home on the first day of the week, the weight of Friday's crucifixion still heavy upon them. Suddenly a stranger joins them in their walk. Their hospitality brings him to their home; there he takes, blesses, breaks, and shares their bread at their table. And in that moment their eyes are opened, and this stranger becomes known to them as the risen Christ (Luke 24:13-35).

John spreads the table in a different way, telling how God's provision of a miraculous catch of fish brings the disciples and the risen Lord around a morning campfire for breakfast. Again, Jesus is the host, taking bread and sharing it, along with the fish. And again, as the meal is shared, recognition occurs (John 21:1-14).

What is striking about these resurrection appearances is that recognition is bound up in nourishment, and nourishment in recognition. Breaking bread, and being fed by it, were central features of the disciples' earliest encounters with the risen Christ. As they were fed, Christ became more clearly revealed, and in that revelation, they were, at the same time, fed. Resurrection has to do with bread shared and Christ encountered, with Christ encountered and bread shared.

To put it another way, the experience of knowing Christ in the power of resurrection is very much like that of having a physical hunger met, of receiving provision for the further enjoyment of life. These are the kinds of experiences of satisfaction and empowerment, of healing and enabling, that are represented in the Easter feast.

We can say, then, that the primary experience of Easter is to be nourished by the risen Lord — inwardly and outwardly, spiritually and physically.[3] In the presence and power of the risen Christ we have the assurance that ours and the world's deepest hungers will be satisfied:

Christ is risen! Shout Hosanna!
Earth and heaven nevermore shall be the same.
Break the bread of new creation
where the world is still in pain.
Tell its grim, demonic chorus:
"Christ is risen! Get you gone!"
God the First and Last is with us.
Sing Hosanna every one![4]

The bread and wine of Holy Communion, shared during Eastertide, are the joyful signs of the gracious, deeply nourishing provision of God, who through the resurrection of Jesus from the dead has begun the renewal, the giving-of-new-life, to all creation. The holy meal serves as a celebration of the good news that "earth and heaven nevermore shall be the same." When we eat the Easter bread and share the cup of resurrection, we participate in that strange and marvelous transformation occurring in us and in our world.

I am reminded of the traditional three-fold interpretation of the meaning of standing to receive communion, a common practice throughout the church's history:[5]

1. We stand as though in haste to partake (as did the Hebrew children at the first Passover).
2. We stand as children confident of their adoption by a loving parent.
3. We stand because we have been raised up with Christ.

To be raised up with Christ is first to meet the risen Christ in faith, and then to be empowered by the Holy Spirit to live new-creation lives — lives of joy, compassion, and reconciliation. The bread and cup of the sacrament are the signs for such an experience of encounter and witness. We approach the table seeking to meet Christ in the breaking of the bread and the feeding of our souls. We leave the table nourished and filled, boldly believing, announcing, and demonstrating with our lives that what God has done in Christ at Easter is only the beginning — all creation shall yet be reborn!

CONCLUSION

The Lord's Table during Eastertide is a place of encountering Christ in the joyful and abundant feast of resurrection. The bread comes from our hands, but then is blessed and shared with us by a host we come to know as the risen Christ. And slowly, wonderment and dim recognition give way to power and witness, and we who have been fed the bread of resurrection and the cup of new creation are set free to go and feed others:

When they had finished breakfast, Jesus said to Simon Peter, "Simon, son of John, do you love me . . .?" He said to him, "Yes, Lord; you know that I love you." Jesus said to him, "Feed my lambs" (John 21:15).

❦ FOR REFLECTION AND DISCUSSION ❧

1. Plan a meal for this session, so that the group comes together without having eaten beforehand. Discuss what your hunger feels like, and how it affects thoughts, moods, actions, and abilities within the group.

2. As you share the meal, consider the resurrection meals referred to in the chapter (Luke 24:28-35, John 21:9-13). Draw comparisons between having the stomach filled and having the spirit filled; between physical satisfaction of hunger and the whole renewal of creation.

3. Ask group members to share an experience in which communion was empowering and renewing, filling an inner need or leading them to experience the resurrected Christ.

4. What are ways communion can better express or emphasize these experiences in our congregational sharing of the sacrament?

5. Refer once again to the two resurrection meal texts (Question 2 above). Note the pattern whereby items of food were provided by disciples, then taken and blessed by Jesus, and offered back to them. Describe experiences within the group of taking something unfinished (such as an unhemmed pair of pants, a canvas oil painting with no frame, a piece of pottery yet to be fired, etc.) and placing it in someone else's hands to complete, then to receive it again in finished form. How is this pattern reflected in our movements and words at the Lord's Table in worship? And in our lives through the Easter experience?

6. Share the Lord's Supper, if this can be arranged.

Study groups proceed to Chapter 8, "Assessment."

6. THE SEASON AFTER PENTECOST OR ORDINARY TIME

*The essential thing "in heaven and in earth" is . . . that
there should be long obedience in the same direction . . .*

FRIEDRICH NIETZSCHE[1]

*They devoted themselves to the apostles' teaching and
fellowship, to the breaking of bread and the prayers.*

ACTS 2:42

THE SEASON AFTER PENTECOST

By now you will have shared the Lord's Table through the two primary cycles of the Christian year — through Advent hope and Christmas joy, through the "beheld" glory of the Epiphany and the "beholden" faith of the season after. You have spread the table in the springtime-wilderness of Lent, and through the great fifty days of Easter and its crown, Pentecost.

Now we come to "Ordinary Time," that marvelous way of referring to the period on the Christian calendar which has no particular biblical point of reference. (As noted in Chapter 3, the season after the Epiphany is also sometimes referred to as Ordinary Time.) Ordinary Time, here known as "the season After Pentecost," is the period of the church year stretching from the Sunday after Pentecost (in May or June) to the beginning of Advent (November or December). On the calendar, it falls more or less opposite the two cycles of Advent, Christmas, Epiphany and Lent, Easter, Pentecost.

Ordinary Time is a time for living through the long stretch with what we have known and believed and seen. The season calls for ordinary faithfulness, or better, for faithfulness in the ordinary things — caring for the family and the fellowship of the church, loving the stranger, laboring for daily bread, witnessing to the faith in word and deed, and worshiping God. It allows the community of faith the opportunity to gather in the myriad lessons and images of the church year as observed to that point, and to spread them out like mown hay laid out to dry in the summer sun.

The Season After Pentecost at the Lord's Table

In such a light, we begin to see certain inner connections in the way bread and cup are shared through the various seasons of communion. Those connections have surely appeared already in the New Testament; from the Emmaus Easter encounter (Luke 24:13ff) we recall the four-fold action (take, bless, break, and share) and its similarities to the actions of another meal held under very different circumstances, the Last Supper (Luke 22:14ff and parallels). And in John's resurrection account of bread and multiplied fish (John 21:1-14) we hear echoes of an earlier day when five loaves and two fish, again given by others into Jesus' hands, fed thousands with plenty to spare (John 6:1ff and parallels). And in that setting, where thousands were fed by the generosity of a child and the miraculous provision of God, we see enacted what Mary sang from deep within the hope-filled season of Advent: "God has filled the hungry with good things . . ." (Luke 1:53).

Through these interwoven references, we can see certain meanings emerge which call for our attention as we share the Lord's Table through Ordinary Time. These various themes have shown themselves to be basic to our study of the Eucharist throughout the seasons of the year. Here I will identify three such themes.

First, the sacramental meal serves to draw those who share it into closer communion with God and one another. This is true in part because of the very nature of sharing bread with another. The word *companion* literally means "with bread," suggesting that our most intimate friends, or co-travelers, are those with whom we break the bread of nourishment and "companionship" along the way. In the Lord's Supper, we renew our communion — our companionship — with God and with the community of the church.

Through participation in the sacrament, the presence of Christ is confirmed and renewed in power and grace, and our fellowship with him is shared with all who gather for this holy meal. In other words, our communion is at once with Christ and with one another. The invocation of the Holy Spirit, which serves as the culmination of the prayer of Great Thanksgiving, draws together both of these meanings of communion: "By your Spirit make us one with Christ, one with each other. . . ."[2]

Second, every time we share the Lord's Table we are reminded of what bread is — food that is intended to nourish, sustain, and strengthen for further living and working. A meal table is not only a place to which we come; it is also a place from which we go. When we share a meal, we are resting from work, but with the same meal we are also preparing for further work.

Some of us may have memories from childhood of parents who, on certain days in particular, wished to feed us a hearty breakfast that would "stick to our ribs." Eating on such occasions was not only an occasion for time together around a table, but — perhaps more important — for preparing to meet a particularly challenging or adventuresome day. To be sure, we share the Eucharist to meet God and to be renewed in our covenant with one another, but we also eat the Lord's Supper to live out whatever follows from that encounter with ample, grace-filled nourishment.

Third, and joining together the above two meanings, the bread broken at the Lord's Table opens out into the world and becomes available to whoever — stranger or friend, foreigner or intimate — happens to be in need of nourishment. A crowd of thousands experienced the provision of God's grace from the hands of Jesus, simply because they were hungry. Strangers were hosted at Sarah and Abraham's table, and turned out to be guests of considerable honor (Genesis 18); so with the Emmaus disciples and their strange guest, and, of course, the messianic figure in one of Jesus' parables who, as a hungry stranger, was nonetheless welcomed and fed by the faithful (Matthew 25:31ff). Jesus brought himself into the homes of many who would have been considered "outside the fold," blending their gifts of bread with his own presence and blessing.

The word *mass*, a traditional Catholic reference to the sacrament, actually derives from the words of dismissal which came at the end of the former Latin liturgy: *et misa est*. Within "the mass," in other words, is contained its own dismissal. The holy meal is intended not only to draw the faithful together, but to scatter them into the world as well.

There is a church in the Middle East whose chancel floor surrounding the communion table is inlaid with designs of fish and loaves. The reference to the feeding of the five thousand comes immediately to mind, with its five loaves and two fish; but there is one difference — the floor design contains two fish, but only four loaves. The fifth is intended to appear on the communion table, and to extend the miracle of feeding into the congregation and the world! The sacrament of Holy Communion is a table for fellowship and communion with God and with God's people; it is a place of nourishment and empowerment for ministry; therefore, it is a table that reaches out beyond the doors of the church building, into the homes of the lonely, the alleys of the homeless, and the hearts of the lost and searching. Our oneness, or communion, with God and with one another is only completed as we move beyond the holy meal to share it with the world in need. Again, the prayer for the Holy Spirit, which contains one more, completing, line: "By your Spirit make us one with Christ, one with each other, and one in ministry to all the world . . ."[3]

The Season After Pentecost includes two special communion days that are worthy of particular mention: World Communion Sunday (observed the first Sunday in October; see *BOW*, pp. 431, 72-73), and All Saints' Day (observed November 1, or the first Sunday following; see *BOW*, pp. 413-15, 74-75). World Communion Sunday, though not a liturgical day, has been observed in many local churches as an occasion of recognizing the universal nature and work of the church as manifested around the world, as well as the church's unity in

Christ. All Saints' Day, a favorite observance for John Wesley, celebrates the lives and memory of the saints who have gone before us, holding up their examples as our inspiration for continuing in lives of faithfulness. The theme of communion with one another in Christ comes strongly to the fore in both of these settings. World Communion Sunday is an occasion to celebrate the rich diversity within that communion; All Saints', to share the holy meal not only as communion, but as sustenance for continuing in joyful labor for the gospel.

Conclusion

"Once upon a time . . ." is the way real life is lived; that is, always upon a time. Whether spectacular or plain, extraordinary or ordinary, faithful life is about moving through time with God and with others, nourished along the way with bread of our hands that is also bread from *God's* hand.

Season after season, year after year, we grow in grace through receiving that consecrated bread, and in the practice of the gospel. We draw near, then scatter to serve, draw near again, then scatter once more — never content to remain at the table, but always eager to return. In such a way we move through the seasons of communion, becoming fashioned over time into the people of God.

Holy time points the way, we might say, so that we are known, not by where we are situated, but by where we are going; not by what we are only, but by what we hope to be, and for the world to be. And the table of the Eucharist provides the feast along the way — always enough, and to spare. There is ample room at that table for quiet, inward reflection as well as open, festive celebration. There is, at the table, the call for preparation and self-examination; and also a word of blessing and thanksgiving. Every holy meal we share contains at once *fulfillment* of new creation and *anticipation* of its coming. Every Sunday is a day of resurrection, yet every communion day we also "proclaim the Lord's death until he comes" (1 Corinthians 11:26). There is an Advent side to every Easter feast.

Such is the nature of the Christian year and of the Table which is shared through it. We glimpse new creation but do not stop and hold that glimpse; we let it go in order to continue moving toward it with our work and our worship. Martin Luther expressed the nature of the journey in an enduring way:

> This life is not righteousness, but growth in righteousness; it is not health, but healing; not being, but becoming; not rest, but exercise; we are not yet what we shall be, but we are growing toward it; the process is not yet finished, but it is going on; this is not the end, but it is the road; all does not yet gleam in glory, but all is being purified.[4]

 ℱ FOR REFLECTION AND DISCUSSION ℱ

1. What is inviting about the word *ordinary*? What is uninviting? Recall experiences in which ordinariness was a positive characteristic.

2. What do you suppose is meant by Neitzsche's phrase, found at the beginning of this chapter, about a "long obedience in the same direction"? Relate this to Luther's words, page 32, about the nature of Christian life.

3. Consider together the three themes related to Holy Communion enumerated in this chapter. Invite group members to share which aspect speaks most directly to them. Which of these would you say are developed more fully in your congregation's communion observances? Less fully?

4. How could these dimensions be filled out, or better balanced, in your congregational worship?

5. Share the Lord's Supper, if this can be arranged.

Study groups proceed to Chapter 8, "Assessment."

PART 2
PLANNING

Introduction

Congregational worship is generally best planned and crafted the same way it is carried out — with others. So, while Part 1 of this workbook may be completed individually, Part 2 is intended for group participation. *The Book of Discipline of The United Methodist Church* mandates that pastors shall "oversee the worship life of the congregation," and that others shall participate with the pastor in that planning process (Paras. 439.1.a and 262.11).

The exercises in this workbook for assessing, planning, and evaluating worship will be most beneficial if they can be undertaken by a "Study Group" with a small "Planning Group" at its core. Ideally, the Planning Group will include the pastor and one or two other worship leaders, and will be a subgroup of the larger Study Group. In this way, individual reflections and group discussions can be used to inform the planning process. Actual planning of services of worship — with all of the specific details that this implies — can then be carried out by the smaller Planning Group while, at the same time, receiving input, direction, and focus from the larger Study Group. Taking this approach, the workbook will lead you along this basic pattern:

1. **Survey:** *Individuals* read and reflect on one of the survey chapters in Part 1, and then meet as a *Study Group* to discuss impressions and insights.

2. **Assessment:** *Individuals* complete the individual exercises in Part 2 (Chapter 7 or 8), and then meet as a *Study Group* to complete the group exercises.

3. **Planning:** *Planning Group* meets to plan the specific service(s) of worship based on directions from the larger Study Group (Chapter 9).

4. **Evaluation:** *Study Group* meets again as a whole to evaluate the service(s) of worship (Chapter 10).

PART 2 LAYOUT

This part of the workbook begins with a "General Local Church Assessment" of your congregation's worship practices (Chapter 7). This general assessment is an exercise to help you become more aware of your congregation's overall observance of Holy Communion. The main question this assessment seeks to answer is, "How do we celebrate Holy Communion?". While all of the materials in this part of the workbook are designed for group use, this particular survey may also be used to poll responses from a range of individuals in your congregation.

Chapter 8 invites you and your Study Group to assess your congregation's observance of communion in a *given season* of the year. The survey questions in this chapter are generic—that is, they can be applied with equal effect to each season of the Christian year. Your answers to the questions, however, will not be generic, for as you think about your own congregation's worship, your answers will reflect specific practices at different times of year (Advent, Christmastide, Lent, etc.). The leading question for this chapter is, "How have we celebrated Holy Communion during this season?". Instructions given with the assessment show which questions need to be completed by individuals prior to class time (in order to facilitate group discussion) and which are to be completed with the group during class.

Chapter 9 is the actual planning module. Again, this is a generic planning module, but the results will not be generic. By working through the questions in the module, your Planning Group will be able to make specific plans for each season of the Christian year. As indicated above, this is designed for use by your 3-5 person Planning Group, not by the larger Study Group as a whole. The leading question for these planning exercises is "How will we celebrate Holy Communion during the approaching season?". Though members of the Planning Group will naturally spend time thinking individually about issues related to the service, the planning module itself is designed to be completed in a group setting with members working together.

Chapter 10 is a process for evaluating the service of worship that you and your Planning Group have implemented. Once again, the Study Group as a whole conducts this evaluation. The question guiding this chapter is: "How was our observance of Holy Communion during the season just experienced?".

For additional suggestions about when and how to schedule Study Groups and Planning Groups for a specific season of the year, see the options outlined in Appendix A, page 79.

OTHER RESOURCES

The two basic worship resources for The United Methodist Church are *The United Methodist Hymnal* and *The United Methodist Book of Worship*. In words borrowed from the *Book of Worship* itself, these two resources are "the cornerstones of United Methodist worship."[1] Therefore, just as survey chapters in Part 1 draw frequently upon hymnody from the *Hymnal*, so Part 2 will utilize both the *Hymnal* and the *Book of Worship* as basic sources for information, direction, and worship resources.

Along with *The United Methodist Hymnal* and *The United Methodist Book of Worship*, two other resources deserve brief mention at this point: Andy Langford's *Blueprints for Worship* and Michael E. Williams' *Preaching Pilgrims*.

Blueprints for Worship is a step-by-step guidebook for preparing for worship. As a companion to the *Hymnal* and to the *Book of Worship*,

Blueprints offers some basic definitions, explanations, and choices regarding local church worship planning. The book also provides planning worksheets on subjects such as baptism, weddings, and the seasons of the Christian year.[2]

In the course of your work, you may also find useful a three-part model found in *Preaching Pilgrims* that Michael Williams recommends for those who preach or who evaluate preaching.[3] This model can be adapted to the planning and evaluation of worship in general. According to this model (adapted for our purposes), planning should include three essential elements:

- The world of the scriptures as reflected in the lectionary for the season
- The world of the members of the congregation who participate in worship
- The world of the planners and worship leaders who guide worship

You will find that the planning modules include a variety of questions that give due attention to each of these three dimensions. Sensitivity to the perspective of each dimension will help you shape a worship liturgy that is at once faithful to the gospel and relevant to contemporary life. (For those who wish to explore this concept in greater detail, Williams' model is further elaborated by Barbara Bate in Appendix B, pages 84-87.)

CONCLUSION

A final word is needed concerning the importance of your task in these pages. Your congregation's worship can never be reduced and evaluated according to a certain set of formulas or categories of measurement. At best, worship resists such formal analysis. As a result, all of your questions, answers, and conclusions will contain a kind of glorious provisionality, reflecting the immeasurable qualities about what we do when we gather to worship God. Keep in mind the objective of the exercises found in this section of the workbook, as stated in the Introduction to Part 1: *To develop understanding and confidence for planning and evaluating sacramental worship in your congregation through the seasons of the Christian year.*

7. GENERAL LOCAL CHURCH ASSESSMENT
"How Do We Celebrate Holy Communion?"

In this chapter you and your Study Group will have the opportunity
to reflect in a general way upon your congregation's observance of Holy
Communion. This exercise is designed to enhance your awareness of your
congregation's basic understanding of and orientation toward the sacrament.
The resulting impressions will serve as a starting point for assessing and
planning worship in specific seasons of the Christian year (Chapter 8). In
keeping with the scheduling suggestions made in Appendix A, you may use this
chapter with Chapter 1, "Introducing the Lord's Table and the Christian Year,"
as a way to get your Study Group off to a good start.

WORKING AS A GROUP

As mentioned before, some parts of this assessment need to be completed
prior to a group meeting so that individuals come to the Study Group ready to
participate. Other parts of the assessment are designed for group process (in
class) requiring no advance preparation. Accordingly, participants will want
to read Chapter 1 (Part 1) and fill in their responses to the exercises (in this
chapter) on A. *Space*, B. *Time*, and C. *Actions* prior to the group meeting.

The *initial meeting* of your Study Group will take about one and a half
hours. Begin with greetings and refreshments as you desire. Then, take about
forty minutes to complete the group process of Exercises D and E. The focus
of these exercises on the use of "Words" in Holy Communion and on personal
experiences should facilitate a good discussion. You will need to have copies of
The United Methodist Hymnal (or other worship resource) available for your
group to use in completing Exercise D.

Once you complete the group exercises, the focus of the meeting can shift
toward the discussion of general impressions and insights. Use the "Focus
Questions" on page 48 to facilitate the discussion. Invite participants to
respond to the focus questions by drawing on their responses to *all* of the
exercises. Based on individual and group responses, does your group seem
to share a general impression of Holy Communion as it is practiced in your
congregation? As participants discuss their thoughts and feelings, some
general patterns will probably begin to emerge. Keep these in mind for later
reference in the seasonal assessments.

DEFINING TERMS

Any process of evaluation or assessment requires establishing some basic terms. When you evaluate a play or a movie, for example, you probably consider features such as length, action, dialogue (script), and feeling. But what factors would you consider in evaluating a service of worship? For our purposes, we shall focus on five terms or features that appear in all services of worship. These terms will be used consistently, both in this general survey and in the seasonal assessments and planning modules that follow.

- *Space* • *Time* • *Actions* • *Words* • *Experience*

Space refers to the visual and other material features of the service. Here we have in mind those dimensions of color, decoration, and placement which, in their own way, work to establish the tone, flow, and direction of the service. Examples are parament and vestment colors, placement of the communion table, and the type of bread and communionware used.

Time refers to how time plays a part — both within the service and in the larger context of the congregation's worship calendar. Here our focus is on the arrangement of actions within the whole, along a temporal frame of reference. Two of the most familiar "time" questions are, "How often is Holy Communion observed in your church?" and "How long is the service of Holy Communion?".

Actions refers to the movement and gestures by presider and congregation which go along with the sacramental observance. Examples are: going to the altar rail for communion, lifting the elements during prayers at the table, and the position of the presider in relation to the table and congregation during the service. This category also suggests the responsive dimension of worship: the places at which our worship leads us into ministry in the world.

With the term *words* we take into account the use of written texts and spoken or verbal language. Examples include written and spoken communion prayers, words of dismissal, liturgical responses, and hymns sung during or around the service of Holy Communion.

Experience is an explicitly subjective measurement, identifying elements related to the worshipers' participation in worship. Experience questions include: "How did you feel during a particular service?", "What emotions did you carry with you from the service?", and "What impressions, insights, or learnings did you derive from it?" We might say that these questions look "within" rather than "around" for their answers.

How the Terms Are Used

Certain questions about *words* and *actions* in worship will certainly overlap with questions about *time, space,* and *experience,* and the reverse is also true. The terms are not to be understood as five blocks lined up in a row, but as interwoven strands of a single cloth.

As you work through the questions in this chapter, keep in mind that impressions are as important as concrete evidence in assessing your church's worship, past and present; that is, generalized recollections — such as remembered emotions, images, or phrases — are just as important as bulletins and prayer texts. Where such impressions and concrete data are combined, all the better.

☙ Assessment ❧

A. Space *(Individuals complete this exercise prior to the group meeting.)*

1. Identify the basic, more or less permanent colors in your sanctuary (walls, flooring, furnishings, etc.).

2. During various seasons and special days, what colors are added to these with fabrics, such as paraments (altar cloths and pulpit cloths) and vestments (e.g., stoles worn by clergy, choir robes, etc.)?

3. What other objects are brought into the sanctuary, or rearranged within it, during certain days or seasons of the year (for example, moving the baptismal font, introducing an Advent wreath, etc.)? Explain.

4. Is your communion table (the table on which the elements are set) free-standing or attached to a wall or other object (such as the pulpit)?

5. While presiding at the table, does the presider stand behind the table, to its side, or in front of it?

6. In terms of communion elements, does your church use a single loaf of bread or wafers?

7. A single cup or individual cups?

8. Describe the communionware used. What materials are the utensils made of (silver, pottery, etc.)?

9. In your own words, what tone or "feel" (festive, somber, formal, etc.) would you say is created by the overall "space" dimension of your congregation's services of communion?

B. Time *(Individuals complete this exercise prior to the group meeting.)*

1. How frequently is Holy Communion observed by your congregation?

2. Within the overall services of worship, how long does the service of Holy Communion generally last?

3. Describe the sense of balance, in terms of energy and attention, between the "Service of the Word" (the scripture readings, sermon, prayers, and other actions that precede communion) and the "Service of the Table" (the ritual of Holy Communion itself).

4. Would you describe the communion service as generally moving slowly, hurriedly, or at a comfortable pace?

5. What is the overall tone or "feel" created by the "time" dimension of your congregation's services of communion?

C. Actions *(Individuals complete this exercise prior to the group meeting.)*

1. Are the communion elements placed on the altar table before worship, or are they presented at some point during the service? Describe the action.

2. Does the congregation generally kneel at the altar rail to receive communion, stand, or remain seated?

3. Is the bread or wafer placed in your hand, or do you take it from a loaf or tray?

4. Does the presider read from a book (such as a hymnal) held by hand, or is a missal (book stand) or the table used for this purpose?

5. Does the presider's presence include certain distinct body movements? (Examples are the raising and lowering of the head; hands lifted outward, upward, or downward in prayer; touching the elements, lifting the elements; and kneeling.) If so, what are some of those gestures?

6. What larger connections, if any, are made during communion between the Lord's Supper and the concrete actions of the congregation in the world (such as feeding the hungry, working for justice, etc.)?

7. What provision, if any, is made to extend communion to those within the fellowship of the congregation who are unable to attend worship?

8. How would you describe the overall tone or "feel" of the services, based upon the whole range of actions involved?

D. Words *(Complete this exercise as a group with hymnals in hand.)*

1. Does your congregation observe communion using a ritual from *The United Methodist Hymnal*, another ritual, or extemporaneous prayers?

2. If you use the *Hymnal*, turn to the front pages of that book. You will find between pages 6 and 31 two basic forms for communion: "Services of Word and Table I-III," and "Service of Word and Table IV." Without consulting past bulletins or other sources, try to identify which of these two forms is your congregation's predominant pattern. Look for words, ordering of prayers, or recognizable phrases that are familiar to you. Note here the service you use most often:

3. Once you have identified your congregation's primary service, make a note of key words or phrases that helped you recognize the text:

4. If your congregation uses another written order, or none at all, ask yourself the same question, either with that printed service in hand, or from memory: What are key words or phrases that help you recall or identify the service as the one your congregation uses?

5. Do these "stand-out" words or phrases indicate anything noteworthy about the tone of the overall communion service? Elaborate.

6. If the text you generally use appears in *The United Methodist Hymnal*, look at that service more closely now. What words or phrases appear to represent the whole; that is, are there key words or phrases you would identify as helping to set the tone or message for the whole communion ritual?

7. Are any parts of your liturgy (such as congregational responses) sung by presider, choir, or congregation? If so, which parts, and how frequently (always, occasionally, etc.)?

8. Is the communion service normally accompanied by particular hymns or special music (solo, choral anthem, or instrumental)? If so, identify selections you can recall.

Permission is granted to copy this page for free distribution in the local church setting.

9. How would you describe the tone of the music sung during or around the communion service (somber, festive, varied, etc.)?

10. Add any additional impressions regarding the overall tone of the "words" dimension of congregational worship on communion Sundays.

E. Experience *(Complete this exercise as a group.)*

1. Recall your earliest memories of Holy Communion.

2. Were these experiences glad? Solemn? Mixed?

3. For what reasons do you think this was so (personal beliefs, external climate of the services, etc.)?

4. Describe your most recent memories of the sacrament.

5. Were these experiences glad? Solemn? Mixed?

6. For what reasons (external and internal) do you think this was so?

7. Complete the following sentences:

   - I believe that receiving communion is a way for us to . . .

   - I believe that receiving communion is a way for God to . . .

   - Preparation for receiving communion involves . . .

   - Some of my thoughts and feelings just after I have received communion are . . .

8. Sharing Holy Communion in our congregation seems to be connected to life in the world a great deal, somewhat, not at all, etc. Explain.

Study Group Focus Questions
For General Assessment

Use these questions to guide group discussion after all exercises are completed.

1. Based on the General Local Church Assessment that you have just completed, how would you say your congregation observes the Lord's Supper? Is Holy Communion in your church setting more an act of quiet reflection or of open celebration? Of introspection or of outward focus? Of remembering or of looking forward?

2. Are there times when Holy Communion includes a mixture of all of these?

3. Does this vary from one season of the year to another?

4. When you leave worship on communion Sundays, do you sense that you have been nourished by the sacrament? In what ways?

5. What makes the Lord's Supper rich and deeply meaningful for you over months and years of time?

6. Individually and as a group, what are your hopes for personal and congregational spiritual nourishment through sharing the Lord's Supper this year?

8. Seasonal Assessment
"How Have We Celebrated Holy Communion During This Season?"

This exercise is designed to be completed after your Study Group has met once to discuss one of the survey chapters from Part 1 of the workbook. For example, if you are preparing to plan for the Advent season, your group will need to complete the survey chapter for Advent (Chapter 2) before beginning the assessment for Advent. Reading the survey chapter first will prepare you to be sensitive as a group to a variety of issues related to the Christian year and to the meanings of Holy Communion. The following dates are recommended for the completion of this sequence in a timely way for each season:

- Advent: Early October
- Christmas, Epiphany: Early November
- Lent: Early January
- Eastertide: Early February
- After Pentecost: Two months prior to service

Working as a Group

Once your Study Group has read, reflected on, and met to discuss the pertinent survey chapter from Part 1, you are ready to undertake the seasonal assessment. Many of the exercises in the assessment will rely on your impressions and remembered perceptions from past worship experiences. You may wish to refer to the "General Church Assessment" in Chapter 7 in order to compare with your further reflections at this point. Answering all of the questions exhaustively is less important than gaining an overall impression of how your congregation worships during the season in view.

Before proceeding, you should make copies of the assessment survey itself, pages 50-57. Since your Study Group will be completing an assessment for each season of the Christian year, you will need to keep a supply of blank copies on hand for future work. Please note that "permission to reproduce" is indicated on these pages.

As in the last chapter, some of the exercises in this assessment are designed to be completed by individual participants prior to the group meeting. The following exercises can be completed in this way in order to facilitate group discussion: Space, Time, Actions.

The first time your Study Group meets to complete a seasonal assessment you may need as much as one and a half hours for your work. In subsequent seasons the assessment should take about one hour. Use the first few minutes of your meeting time for greetings, prayers, and refreshments as you desire. Then, take about forty minutes to complete the group process of Exercises D and E. For these exercises you will need to have copies of bulletins and worship notes from the previous year's seasonal service, as well as copies of *The United Methodist Hymnal* and *The United Methodist Book of Worship*.

Once you have completed the group exercises, the meeting can move forward with specific suggestions for those who will be charged with planning. Use the "Focus Questions" on page 58 to recall areas where you want to make suggestions. Encourage participants to draw on their responses to *all* of the other assessment exercises. The suggestions may be of a generalized sort, or very specific, concerning a particular matter of some detail. The primary goal is to communicate your Study Group's basic vision or desire for worship during the season in view. From there, your Planning Group will take the next step in implementing the vision.

❧ ASSESSMENT ❧

A. Space *(Individuals complete this exercise prior to the group meeting.)*

1. Think about the appearance of your sanctuary in the season you are studying. Recall the appearance of your sanctuary during this season in past years. As this season begins, does the appearance of the sanctuary change? Note such changes here and on the following page, including changes in colors, cloths, objects, etc. For information about colors and other features appropriate to the respective seasons, see the seasonal chapter introductions in *The Book of Worship*, as well as the articles on "Colors for the Christian Year" (page 226) and "The Christian Year" (page 224).

2. Is the communion table placed so that the presider stands behind it, facing the people? (See *BOW*, pp. 28-29).

3. A loaf of bread and chalice suggest many different themes in each season. For example, in a season of hungering (Advent), a tangible loaf and cup are palpable symbols of promise. In a season of feasting (Christmastide), they are signs of the fullness and richness of the season. In Lent, they suggest nourishment given along the journey toward Jerusalem. An unleavened loaf and a simple cup also provide a visual association with the Passover meal. In the scriptures associated with Easter, bread is mentioned frequently and is a sign of new life and renewed fellowship. And during Ordinary Time, the bread and cup are symbols of abundance and daily nourishment. What form does the bread of communion take in your communion worship during the season you have in view?

4. In terms of communionware, how has the wine or grape juice been served (from a common cup or in individual cups)?

5. Taking into account your own local setting, what other ways have you used or might you use to emphasize the respective themes of the season in your worship space?

B. Time *(Individuals complete this exercise prior to the group meeting.)*

1. Continue to think about the past experiences and customs of your congregation. Focusing specifically on the last year or two, when was Holy Communion celebrated during the season in view?

    _____ The first Sunday of the month?
    _____ Weekly?
    _____ Other special gatherings?

2. Was the service abbreviated or did it include the full liturgy (such as the ones found on pp. 12-16 in the *Hymnal*)?

3. Describe the sense of balance (proportion), in terms of energy and attention, between the "Service of the Word" (that which precedes communion) and the "Service of the Table" (communion and all that follows).

4. In addition to Sunday morning worship, each season offers special opportunities for gathering around the Lord's Table. Consider, for example:

- *Advent* — a festival of lessons and carols
- *Christmastide* — Christmas Eve, las posadas, covenant renewal service, watch night, and baptismal reaffirmation (see *BOW*, pp. 269ff; pp. 299-301; p. 111)
- *Lent* — Ash Wednesday, services of healing, Passion or Palm Sunday, and Holy Thursday (*BOW*, pp. 320ff; 615ff)
- *Easter* — Easter vigil, Easter evening, and the day of Pentecost (*BOW*, pp. 368ff)
- *After Pentecost* — Bible studies, a Council on Ministries retreat, and outdoor evening vespers

Does your congregation celebrate Holy Communion on any of these or other occasions during the season you are studying? Which ones?

C. Actions *(Individuals complete this exercise prior to the group meeting.)*

1. In last year's service for the season you are considering, were communion elements brought forward during the service, or placed on the altar table beforehand (see *BOW*, p. 26)?

2. The way the elements are brought forward as part of the offertory can give expression to themes of the various seasons of the year; for example:

- *Advent* — giving ourselves and our lives to God in preparation for God's coming
- *Christmastide* — the biblical witness of shepherds, magi, and others who presented their gifts to the Christ child
- *Lent* — the intention of self-offering in preparation for Easter
- *Easter* — participation in the renewal of creation in tangible signs of bread and wine
- *Ordinary Time* — the presentation of the fruits of our labors in harvest

Has your congregation developed any special ways of bringing the elements forward in the season you are considering?

3. During last year's service, did the congregation receive communion kneeling, standing, or sitting? Differently on different occasions?

4. Consider how congregational postures for receiving communion (kneeling, standing, sitting) can affect and support the themes and attitudes of the season. Write your thoughts here.

(As the Planning Group plans worship in the pages ahead, a choice will need to be made among these postures, based upon the primary themes of the day or season and other factors. If the sacrament is to be shared more than once during the season, you may wish to vary the method of receiving. See *BOW*, p. 29 for further direction.)

5. What larger connections, if any, have been made during communion services between the Lord's Supper and the concrete needs of the congregation and of the world?

6. What provision, if any, has been made to share the eucharistic meal with those within the fellowship of the congregation who are unable to attend worship?

the actions of nos. 5 or 6 above could be initiated

exercise as a group with hymnals and past worship

more orders of worship from a communion Sunday
son. Which liturgy of communion in *The United*
as used?

d at the table of Holy Communion which were
ason and themes of this season? Explain.

3. How was the time during which communion was being shared observed by the congregation? In silence, singing, instrumental music, choral music? Note specific hymn or special music texts normally used during this time:

4. Do the written texts and spoken language within the communion liturgy, such as the Prayer of Great Thanksgiving and congregational hymns sung during and around communion, express themes of the season?

5. Are there opportunities for singing during communion (such as Great Thanksgiving prayer responses, hymns during serving, etc.) that might offer an occasion to develop further the themes of the day? Note some of these instances.

E. Experience *(Complete this exercise as a group.)*

1. Describe your thoughts and feelings or dispositions as you moved through a service of communion during this season of the year.

2. How did the elements of space, time, and actions, as they've been examined above, contribute to these experiences?

7. Are there ways in which the actions of nos. 5 or 6 above could be initiated or improved?

D. Words *(Complete this exercise as a group with hymnals and past worship bulletins in hand.)*

1. Look through one or more orders of worship from a communion Sunday during last year's season. Which liturgy of communion in *The United Methodist Hymnal* was used?

2. Were prayers offered at the table of Holy Communion which were particular to the season and themes of this season? Explain.

3. How was the time during which communion was being shared observed by the congregation? In silence, singing, instrumental music, choral music? Note specific hymn or special music texts normally used during this time:

4. Do the written texts and spoken language within the communion liturgy, such as the Prayer of Great Thanksgiving and congregational hymns sung during and around communion, express themes of the season?

5. Are there opportunities for singing during communion (such as Great Thanksgiving prayer responses, hymns during serving, etc.) that might offer an occasion to develop further the themes of the day? Note some of these instances.

E. Experience *(Complete this exercise as a group.)*

1. Describe your thoughts and feelings or dispositions as you moved through a service of communion during this season of the year.

2. How did the elements of space, time, and actions, as they've been examined above, contribute to these experiences?

3. Below is a list of words or themes used in the survey chapters to describe the tone or theological perspective of the season being discussed:

   - *Advent* — hunger, yearning, preparation, expectation, hope, anticipation, waiting
   - *Christmastide* — Messiah's birth, shepherds, magi, celebration, feasting, glory, renewal, reaffirmation
   - *Lent* — humility, yearning, preparation, waiting, surrender
   - *Easter* — joy, new creation, witness, transformation, power, feasting
   - *Ordinary Time* — faithfulness, witnessing, worshiping, companionship with God and with others, labor

   How well do the words listed above describe your own communion experience during the season you are studying?

4. Which of these words or themes would you like to see included more intentionally in planning sacramental worship for the season?

5. Are there other words or themes that could use emphasis in your particular setting?

Study Group Focus Questions
For Seasonal Assessment

Review all exercises for suggestions to the Planning Group.

1. Share some of your own wishes or expectations for personal and congregational spiritual growth through the setting of eucharistic worship during this season.

2. What themes would you like to see included more intentionally in planning worship for the season?

3. Prepare three short, affirmative sentences that you would want to be spoken by a person leaving the service:
   - God . . .
   - I/We . . .
   - The world . . .

4. Are there certain congregational elements — a piece of history, a special hymn or prayer, a color or symbol with special meaning in your congregation — that you feel would help to express seasonal themes in your local church?

5. What other items related to space, time, actions, words, or experience do you think need attention in worship planning for this season?

6. State any other ideas or concerns for the service that you would like to see considered in the planning process.

The results of this discussion can now be handed along to your Planning Group for use in its work. The Planning Group will use Chapter 9 as a guide for designing the worship service(s). The Study Group will pick its work up again with the evaluation of the service(s) in Chapter 10.

9. Seasonal Planning
"How Will We Celebrate Holy Communion This Year?"

This chapter is designed for use by a small Planning Group. As mentioned before, ideally, this group will include the pastor and two or three other worship leaders, and will function as a subgroup to represent the vision of your Study Group. Your task is to plan the various specific elements of one or more services of worship for a particular season of the year. You come to your task equipped with a variety of raw materials. As you proceed, keep in mind your learnings from the pertinent survey chapter in Part 1. Use the findings of your Study Group made available from the Seasonal Assessment (Chapter 8). Pay special attention to the directions handed along with the "Focus Questions" in that chapter. The following dates are recommended for the completion of planning in a timely way for each season:

- Advent: Early October
- Christmas, Epiphany: Early November
- Lent: Early January
- Eastertide: Early February
- After Pentecost: Two months prior to service

Working as a Group

As a Planning Group, you will need approximately one and a half hours to complete the planning module that follows. Before proceeding, you should make copies of the planning module itself, pages 61-68. For the planning process to continue with other seasons of the Christian year, you will need a supply of blank copies on hand for future work. Please note that the publisher has granted permission to copy these pages for free distribution in the local church setting.

The Three Worlds

As you begin your work, remember to include in your planning both the formal, traditional dimensions of worship, and any local congregational elements that help to express the themes of the day in your particular setting. Let these two expressions, along with your own creative input — what we have called the "three worlds" — blend together to form your plan for sacramental worship during this season. You will see questions from each of these perspectives in the pages ahead. Sensitivity on your part to the perspective of each dimension will help you shape a worship liturgy that is at once faithful to the gospel and relevant to the life of your congregation. (You may wish to refer once again to the Introduction to Part 2, pages 36-38, for a brief explanation of this model, as well as to Appendix B.)

Scripture, Hymns, and Prayers

The Revised Common Lectionary is a selection of scripture readings for each Sunday of the year. As such, the *Lectionary* lends substantial help in selecting biblical texts that are pertinent to the focus and emphasis of the service you are planning. (For a complete *Lectionary* listing, see *Book of Worship*, pp. 227ff.) For our purposes, the planning module that follows will assume the use of the *Lectionary*.

One of the tried-and-true principles of the best worship planning is to select hymns, prayers, greetings, and other special music that fit with the scripture texts for the day. The "Index of Scripture" in *The United Methodist Hymnal* (pp. 923-26) provides a reference list linking scripture texts with hymns, services, etc.

Congregational prayers can be found in a variety of sources including the *Hymnal*, the *Book of Worship*, other books of collected prayers, and prayers written specifically for the service you are planning. (Writing congregational prayers is challenging work, but it can be very worthwhile. Some of the most meaningful prayers in the life of a congregation come directly out of its experience as articulated by one or two persons.) Eucharistic prayers for each season can be found in the Book of Worship in the section entitled "Services of Word and Table" (pp. 54-80).

Introducing Changes into Worship

Another tested rule of worship planning is to use wisdom when introducing new or unfamiliar elements into worship. If you plan to introduce new gestures or congregational acts, different kinds of bread or methods of serving communion, changes in colors or textures displayed, take time deciding how and when to introduce them. An announcement prior to the beginning of worship is one option, with the presider or another worship leader explaining the changes. Other options are an article in the church newsletter or a statement in the previous Sunday's announcements or bulletin. Most important, however, is that worshipers be prepared for changes, understand their significance, and, as a consequence, not be surprised and possibly confused by them.

Distraction is a normal side-effect of change; don't let this keep you from exploring new ways to grasp and express ancient meanings. Repetition and the passing of time can bring familiarity, acceptance, and appreciation.

A FINAL WORD ABOUT WORSHIP PLANNING

We cannot, in actuality, plan worship; we can only plan *services* of worship. Worship happens, not by prescribed words and movements, however well these may be arranged, but by the moving of the Spirit in a specific place, at a specific time, with a specific group of worshipers. Your task will be to weave together the various elements of worship and to present them as your own gift to God shared through the congregation. Prayer is always an appropriate way to begin such a task.

❦ PLANNING MODULE ❦

A. Space

For some additional ideas about suggested colors, textures, and other implements, see the introductory articles that appear with each season in *The Book of Worship*, as well as the general comments on pages 224 and 226.

1. What colors, implements, fabrics, and textures, will be chosen for the sanctuary for the season in view? Examples are the Advent wreath, the Chrismon tree, and the color blue for Advent; the nativity crèche, baptismal font, and water jars for Christmas, Epiphany; a wooden cross, basin and towel, or a rough-hewn cloth for Lent; and a Christ candle for Easter.

2. What local history, artisans, or other contextual features might illumine the meaning of the colors and other items selected?

3. Will banners be prepared, or hung if already prepared? Which seasonal themes do these banners express?

4. Will a loaf of bread be used, or wafers (see *BOW*, pp. 28-29)?

5. Individual cups or a common cup?

6. If your congregation is not accustomed to using a loaf of bread, what symbolic benefit might be achieved by introducing this practice on a trial basis?

7. What benefit might be achieved by introducing a common cup?

8. Is the table situated so that the presiding pastor can stand behind it (*BOW*, pp. 28-29)? If not, what is the desired significance of where the presider stands?

B. Time

1. When will the Eucharist be shared in worship during the season? Which Sundays?

2. Which special days?

3. On communion Sundays, will the full eucharistic liturgy be used?

4. If so, will other aspects of the service need to be adjusted for the sake of time, or will the service simply be longer?

C. Actions

1. Will your service(s) include a processional? If so, describe how this action will express the themes of the season.

2. Will communion elements be brought forth and placed on the altar table as part of the offertory (*BOW*, p. 26)? If so, how will this action be undertaken?

3. Considering the themes of the service, how will the congregation receive the elements (standing, kneeling, or sitting)?

4. Are there other gestures or movements that would help your congregation express the themes of the season? Elaborate.

5. In the service you are planning, how might the larger connection between the Eucharist and the concrete needs of the local community and the world, or congregational needs and hungers, be made tangible in the service?

6. What provision will be made to share the eucharistic meal with those within the fellowship of the congregation who are unable to attend worship[1] (see *BOW*, pp. 51ff; *Book of Discipline*, Para 1217.9)?

D. Words

1. Beginning with scripture, choose the texts that will establish the focus and emphasis of the service. (See *Book of Worship*, pp. 227ff, for a full *Lectionary* listing; then find the texts for the Sunday under consideration.) Themes for preaching can be obtained from the pastor. If the pastor plans to use scriptures outside the lectionary, include these texts in the further shaping of the service.

   - Gospel text:
   - Epistle text:
   - Old Testament text:
   - Psalm:

2. State the theme for preaching, worship, and communion in one brief, affirmative sentence.

3. Now select the hymns and other special music that follow the scriptural focus for the day. In *The United Methodist Hymnal*, refer to the sections of hymns related to various seasons of the year, e.g., "Promised Coming" (pp. 195-216) for Advent; "Birth and Baptism" (pp. 217-55) and "Life and Teaching" (pp. 256-78) for Christmas and Epiphany, etc. Explore these and other sections of the *Hymnal* for hymns appropriate to the particular service you are planning. The "Index of Scripture" (pp. 923-26) also provides a reference list linking scripture texts with hymns, services, and other texts. The "Index of Topics and Categories" (pp. 934ff) provides additional thematic referencing of hymns. Which hymns best express the themes you have chosen for the service?

4. The "Eucharist" section of the *Hymnal* (pp. 612-41) provides a range of communion hymns. Can you select a eucharistic hymn that fits with the themes of the day?

5. See the *Book of Worship* (pp. 54-80) for eucharistic prayers for each season. Choose a prayer appropriate to the scripture texts, hymns, and themes selected.

6. Will certain prayer responses be sung? If so, which settings will be used?

7. Considering the themes you have chosen for the service, how will the time during which communion is served be observed by the congregation? In silence? With music? With singing? (See *BOW*, p. 30.)

If music or singing is involved during serving, what hymns or special music will be used?

What additional prayers will be used?

What choral music will be used?

E. Experience

1. What emotions do you hope to evoke through the service of worship?

2. What impressions do you want worshipers to carry with them from the service?

3. The gospel presents us with both "gift" and "task," both blessing and calling. What will be the "gift" presented and experienced in this service?

4. What will be the "task"?

5. Prepare three short, affirmative sentences that would, ideally, be spoken by a person leaving the service:

   * God . . .
   * I/We . . .
   * The world . . .

6. Review the choices you made in Sections A through D above. Which elements may need further refinement in order to fulfill the heart of your plan?

7. MISCELLANEOUS PLANNING NOTES:

10. SEASONAL EVALUATION
"How Was Our Observance of Holy Communion This Year?"

You have now experienced sacramental worship as a "participant observer" in a particular season of the Christian year. You have helped plan the service. You may also have helped lead the service. In either case, you are now ready to evaluate the service in terms of its overall faithfulness to the themes and objectives that you and your Study Group set forth. Evaluating the service will require sharing impressions, voicing observations and perceptions, then sharpening these with feedback from other members of the group. Work toward an integrated evaluation, but expect diversity at this point. You and your group will sometimes have differing views. The very quality of amplitude in the service suggests that worshipers and planners will bring a variety of impressions!

WORKING AS A GROUP

The evaluation meeting is designed for all members of the Study Group. (The Planning Group once again takes its place as a subgroup within the larger team.) The meeting should take place during the week following the service and should last about an hour. Before proceeding, be sure to make copies of the evaluation questions (pages 70-77) so that you will have additional blank copies to use in the future. Please note again that the publisher has granted permission to copy these pages for use with this study.

Evaluation in this setting employs much the same method and works at the same level as the initial study of your congregation's worship practices (Chapter 7). Here, however, impressions and "readings" are likely to be more readily available — and perhaps more helpful, since they are emerging in such close proximity to the actual experience of planning and witnessing the service. All of the questions on the evaluation are designed to be completed by individuals prior to the group meeting (with a copy of the worship bulletin in hand). Use the "Focus Questions" on page 78 to guide group discussion and to make suggestions for next year's Study and Planning Group.

❧ Evaluation ❧

All exercises in this evaluation are designed to be completed by individuals prior to the group meeting.

A. Space

1. How well did the objects and visual materials of worship (communion elements, communionware, colors, placement of the communion table) serve the themes and objectives of the service?

2. In what ways did these physical objects convey meanings on their own?

3. Were there contradictory elements among them, such as colors or objects that did not fit within the whole tone or movement of the service?

4. What would you identify as the most positive or helpful spatial aspects of the service?

5. What would you change in future planning?

B. Time

1. Describe the sense of balance (proportion), in terms of energy and attention, between the "Service of the Word" (that which precedes Holy Communion) and the "Service of the Table."

2. Was the service of communion well placed in the season, or would you have scheduled this differently?

3. What would you identify as positive temporal aspects of the service?

4. What would you change in future planning?

C. Actions

1. How well did movements and gestures fit with the words and feel of the service?

2. Can you point to a change in movements or gestures by presider or congregation (such as lifting hands behind the table during prayers, bringing forward the communion elements as offertory acts, standing to receive, etc.) that added to the texture and richness of the service?

3. Were there any actions or movements that detracted from the service? If so, what were these?

4. If any special fellowship or community events, meals, etc., were planned, how did these enhance or underscore the meanings of Holy Communion that you were hoping for the congregation to share in this season?

5. If the eucharistic meal was shared with those unable to attend worship, how was this received?

6. What would you identify as positive "movement" aspects of the service?

7. What would you change in future planning?

D. Words

1. How would you restate the theme, not as planned, but as heard and experienced through participation in the service?

2. Does this correspond to the theme as planned? How so, or how not?

3. If there was variance, was this a positive shift, or not?

4. Was the fit among scripture, sermon, prayers, and hymns complementary, contradictory, or some of both? Elaborate.

5. Did the service as a whole, including hymns, prayers, and sermon, express the seasonal themes as intended? If so, how so? If not, identify reasons for this.

6. The gospel presents us with both "gift" and "task," both blessing and calling to responsibility. In what ways was each communicated verbally in this service of worship?

7. What would you identify as positive verbal aspects of the service?

8. What would you change in future planning?

E. Experience

1. What was the message you heard and experienced through the communion service? Sum this up in one brief, affirmative sentence:

2. What was, for you, the single most important part of the service, and why?

3. How did communion complement, contrast with, or detract from other actions, themes, and emotions of the service?

4. Was one theme so dominant and often repeated that no other meanings were able to surface, or did the principal theme or set of themes leave room for other expressions, dimensions, and experiences?

5. If you had been a first-time visitor to the church, how do you imagine you would have experienced the service?

6. Of the "three worlds" mentioned in the Introduction and at the beginning of Part 2 (1. the world of scripture, 2. the world of the congregation, 3. the world of the worship planners and leaders), was any too dominant or recessive? Explain.

7. What would you need to do in the future to strike a better balance among the three?

8. What would you identify as positive experiential aspects of the service?

9. What would you change in future planning?

Study Group Focus Questions
For Seasonal Evaluation

Review all exercises for impressions and ideas for next year's Study Group.

1. What surprised you in the service in a positive way?

2. What caught you by surprise in a disappointing way?

3. If significant changes occurred (such as introducing a common cup, or certain gestures), how did you and others receive these changes?

4. Were changes introduced with adequate care and explanation? Elaborate.

5. If you could plan the service again, what would you change?

6. What would you keep?

7. If members of the group experienced the service in different ways, how might these differences be used to enrich future planning?

8. Notes for next year's Study Group:

   - Space:

   - Time:

   - Actions:

   - Words:

   - Experience:

   - General:

APPENDIX A
Suggested Schedules
For Worship Planning

Worship planning can be scheduled in many ways. The most appropriate schedule for meeting and planning depends in large part on the size and purpose of your group. If your group is interested only in discussion (not in actual planning), then a discussion format is all you need. Schedule 1, page 80, is designed for a *Discussion Group*.

If your group is interested in planning services of worship, then you will need to create a *Study Group* with a small *Planning Group* at its core (see page 48). The members of this combined group will work together to assess, plan, experience, and evaluate one or more actual services of worship. Planning and evaluating worship naturally takes additional time and commitment. Schedules 2-4 below present several formats for completing the essential tasks.

No matter which format for planning you select, you will want to complete your plan in a timely way for each season. If you complete your plans by the following dates, you'll be in good time for each season of the Christian year.

- **Advent:** Early October
- **Christmas, Epiphany:** Early November
- **Lent:** Early January
- **Eastertide:** Early February
- **After Pentecost:** Two months prior to service

⇥ SCHEDULE 1 ⇤
Discussion Group

The basic schedule for a *Discussion Group* includes reading and discussing all five of the survey chapters (Chapters 2-6). Since the model involves no planning or evaluation of actual services of worship, it can be used in any setting or season.

FIRST SESSION *(1 hour)*

- *Leader* introduces the subject using Chapter 1, "Introducing the Lord's Table and the Christian Year."

- *Group* discusses initial impressions of the material.

FIVE SUBSEQUENT SESSIONS *(1 hour each)*

- *Individuals* read and reflect on survey chapters, one each week for five weeks.

- *Group* discusses personal responses to the "Questions for Reflection and Discussion" that appear with each chapter.

→ SCHEDULE 2 ←

Weeknight Sequence
For Study and Planning Group

(Includes General Local Church Assessment)

This schedule is for a *Study and Planning Group*. The model begins in late September in order to complete planning by early October. This is an effective timeline for Advent planning. To transpose the model to another season, simply plug in the recommended dates for completing the "Planning Module" (as given above).

FIRST SESSION *(2 hours)* Late September

- *Individual Preparation:* Read "Introduction" to Part 1, and all of Chapter 1, "Introducing the Lord's Table and the Christian Year." Complete the individual exercises of the "General Local Church Assessment" (Chapter 7).

- *Study Group:* Complete Exercises D and E (group process) of the "General Local Church Assessment" (Chapter 7). Use the "Focus Questions" (page 48) to discuss Chapter 1 and other responses to the general assessment.

SECOND SESSION *(2 hours)* Early October

- *Individual Preparation:* Individual Preparation: Read Chapter 2, "The Season of Advent." Focusing on Advent, complete the individual exercises of the "Seasonal Assessment," Chapter 8.

- *Study Group:* Complete Exercises D and E (group process) of the "Seasonal Assessment." Use the "Focus Questions" (page 58) to discuss Chapter 2 and other responses to this assessment.

THIRD SESSION *(1 1/2 hours)* Early October

- *Planning Group:* Plan for Advent by completing the "Planning Module" (Chapter 9).

FOURTH SESSION *(1 1/2 hours)* The week following the service

- *Study Group:* Evaluate the Advent service by completing the "Seasonal Evaluation" (Chapter 10).

⇥ SCHEDULE 3 ⇤
Retreat Sequence
For Study and Planning Group
(Includes General Local Church Assessment)

Like Schedule 2, this model is for a *Study and Planning Group*. Once again, the suggested timeline for Advent can be transposed to another season simply by plugging in the dates recommended on page 59.

FIRST SESSION *(2 hours)* Friday P.M.

- *Individual Preparation:* At home or on retreat, read the "Introduction" to Part 1 and all of Chapters 1 and 2 — "Introducing the Lord's Table and the Christian Year" and "The Season of Advent." Complete the individual exercises of the "General Local Church Assessment," as well as the individual exercises of the "Seasonal Assessment" (Chapter 8) — the latter with the focus on Advent.

- *Study Group:* Complete Exercises D and E (group process) of the "General Local Church Assessment." Use the "Focus Questions" (page 48) to discuss Chapter 1 and other responses to the general assessment.

SECOND SESSION *(2 hours)* Saturday A.M.

- *Study Group:* Complete Exercises D and E (group process) of the Advent assessment (Chapter 8), and use the "Focus Questions" (page 58) to discuss Chapter 2 and other responses to this assessment.

THIRD SESSION *(1 1/2 hours)* Saturday P.M.

- *Planning Group:* Complete the "Planning Module" (Chapter 9) for Advent.

FOURTH SESSION *(1 hour)* The week following the service

- *Study Group:* Complete the "Seasonal Evaluation" (Chapter 10).

✈ SCHEDULE 4 ✦
Mini-Retreat
For Study and Planning Group
(Assumes General Local Church Assessment)

Again, this model is for a *Study and Planning Group*. Plug in appropriate dates for each season as needed.

FIRST SESSION *(2 hours)* Friday P.M.

- *Individual Preparation:* Prior to arriving at the retreat site, read Chapter 2, "The Season of Advent," and complete the individual exercises of the "Seasonal Assessment" (Chapter 8).

- *Study Group:* Complete Exercises D and E (group process) of the "Seasonal Assessment," and use the "Focus Questions" (page 58) to discuss all responses.

SECOND SESSION *(1 1/2 hours)* Saturday A.M.

- *Planning Group:* Complete the "Planning Module" (Chapter 9).

THIRD SESSION *(1 hour)* The week following the service

- *Study Group:* Complete the "Seasonal Evaluation" (Chapter 10).

APPENDIX B
The Three Worlds
In Worship Planning

INTRODUCTION

The following appendix was prepared by Barbara Bate, General Board of Discipleship staff, for the purpose of further illuminating in a worship planning context the three-worlds model found in Michael E. Williams' Preaching Pilgrims. *The model is referred to briefly on page 37 of this workbook and is implied throughout, in all of the exercises. Further ideas on the subject can be found in Barbara Bate's curriculum guide for the lay speaking advanced course,* Lay Speakers Preach *(also available from Discipleship Resources).*

Paul L. Escamilla

When we come together in worship, we bring to that event our own stories, our circumstances, and our understandings of the biblical accounts of God's people. It can be helpful to think of worship as an encounter of human joys, struggles, and yearnings for closeness with God, within a nurturing community striving to be faithful in discipleship. The visual model below portrays this meeting or encounter as the intersection of three worlds: the world of the biblical scriptures, the world of the congregation and its wider community, and the world of the worship planners as interpreters of tradition and experience.

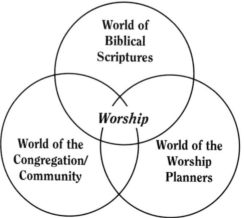

This model portrays worship as a holy moment of intersection for all three of the worlds we bring with us into Christ's presence. Christians are supported first by the knowledge of the biblical history and witness to God's unending commitment to humanity. Whether people were being called "Israel," "The Way," or "the disciples," the biblical accounts embody the wonderfully earthy and concrete stories of people whose lives took radical turns when they met the Holy One. These stories continue to both delight and challenge adults and children. They can prevent your congregation and you as leaders from becoming "other-worldly" either in or out of worship. The scriptural world offers a perspective on life as God intends for it to be lived, with a commitment to love and justice for all people and gratitude for God's everlasting faithfulness to us.

The congregation, and the community in which it finds itself, form another world of experience which you as worship planners have as a resource for your planning. Each congregation has a unique history. Many, though not all, have a central focus of mission and ministry that guides their approach to every decision or opportunity. Some congregations see themselves as prophetic witnesses to a surrounding urban area; some view themselves as nurturing young individuals or families who are new to Christianity; some celebrate their particular gifts in musical expression; some extend a particular welcome to persons recovering from pain, abuse, or addiction. Whatever the predominant self-portrayal or focus of your congregation, it offers a major gift for you to affirm during worship. At the same time, you have the responsibility of encouraging your congregation to expand its awareness and its potential for ministry beyond allegiance to any single approach. This responsibility is expressed in the model by the areas in which each of the three circles meets one of the others. Love of music, for example, without a consciousness of the biblical call to both praise and repentance, would make your worship less than faithful.

The world of the worship planners is clearly affected by the experiences of each of the persons involved. But there is a reality beyond individual personality and talents that is being affirmed in the wider church. In 1992 the General Conference of The United Methodist Church added language to *The Book of Discipline* (paragraph 262.11a) that calls for cooperative worship planning in local congregations on a regular basis. Underlying these words is an important understanding of leadership in the local church. When pastors are not expected to have all the insight and all the resources for developing worship, they become less isolated from parishioners and freer to express concerns, to listen to others' insights, and to test ideas and approaches in a setting of mutual trust and empowerment. This book as a whole is based on the confidence that spiritual leadership emerges from a gathering of caring people. Planning the Lord's Supper is thus a microcosm of the gathering at the Table itself. Worship planners can help bring about a worship experience that reveals a joint vision, reflecting both scriptural and congregational realities, rather than a "scrapbook service" of unconnected parts.

When you plan a worship service, you are making choices about rhythm and theme, about levels of formality, about the use of time and space, and ultimately about what to include and exclude from your congregation's worship. Becoming aware of the values and assumptions behind any of these choices will help you communicate more effectively as part of a worship planning team. The three worlds of experience shown in the three-part model can remind you that all three worlds are essential to lifegiving, creative worship. Omitting or de-emphasizing any one of the three will make your planning shortsighted and its results less faithful to the empowering presence of God with God's people.

Here are some questions you can ask as you consider each of the worlds of experience in your worship planning process.

1. **Regarding the world of the scriptures:**

   a. Where can the stories of biblical people be experienced concretely in your worship service?

   b. What kinds of biblical words and phrases will be woven into the service?

   c. Where are the essential biblical ideas or themes embodied in the ways your worship will be done? (For example, in terms of the Lord's Supper, you may want to address the proportions of judgment and grace, mourning and celebration, gratitude and shame in your local church's observance.)

2. **Regarding the world of the congregation and community:**

   a. What are your congregation's expressed views or implied attitudes toward the Lord's Supper?

   b. What are the barriers or "fences" around the Lord's Table — tradition, physical arrangement, other facets of your community's history and expectations?

   c. Who participates in the Lord's Supper, in leadership, in extending it to persons in the pews, in taking the Lord's Supper to persons who cannot be present on Sunday morning?

3. **Regarding the world of the worship planners:**

   a. What excites you most personally about worship? What fails to keep your own energy and interest strong? What can you, as part of a worship planning team, do to address that concern?

   b. What are your beliefs about the range and variety of worship elements — music, prayer, dance or visual arts — that are appropriate for Sunday worship, or for particular seasons of worship?

   c. What gifts and talents do you bring into the team of people planning worship services in your church? Hymn #87 in the 1989 *United Methodist Hymnal*, "What Gift Can We Bring?," written by Jane

Marshall for a local congregation's anniversary celebration, offers a wonderful set of images for thinking about your congregation's heritage and witness.

d. What areas of hesitation do you now have that can become opportunities for growth in your own leadership?

e. (*Particularly if you are a pastor*) How do you see worship planning — in terms of the priesthood of all believers, as a professional skill about which you will be evaluated, as a journey into unknown territories for the work of the Spirit?

f. In what ways can the conversations that serve the cooperative planning process in your church be strengthened?

Discussing in a worship planning group your thoughts about each of these three worlds can be a creative, constructive way to increase your own understanding of worship as liturgy, "the work of the people."

You have the chance each time you celebrate the Lord's Supper to renew your own commitment to the primary task of the local church. You are called to welcome people into the fellowship of the Table, to deepen their certainty that they are connected to God in Christ, to nurture and feed them within a loving community, and to send them forth strengthened for the work of discipleship in the world. The holy moment of worship can bring forth the amazing energies of God's Spirit with the help of your own care in planning that worship together.

BARBARA BATE
General Board of Discipleship

≋ ENDNOTES ≋

PART 1

Introduction
1Paraphrased from Hugh Kenner, *The Pound Era* (Berkeley, CA: University of California Press, 1971), p. 39. © 1971 Hugh Kenner. Used with permission.

Chapter 1
1Pius Parsch, *The Church's Year of Grace*, Vol. 1 (Collegeville, MN: The Liturgical Press, 1967), pp. 5-6. Used with permission.

2"A Service of Word and Table II," *The United Methodist Hymnal* (Nashville: The United Methodist Publishing House, 1989), p. 14. From "An Order of Sunday Worship Using the Basic Pattern" © 1985, 1989 The United Methodist Publishing House. Reprinted from *The United Methodist Hymnal* with permission.

Chapter 2
1Anthony J. Padovano, *Dawn Without Darkness* (New York: Doubleday & Co., Inc., 1982), pp. 11-12. © 1982 Anthony J. Padovano. Used with permission.

2Selected references: Genesis 7; Exodus 16:35, 24:18, 34:28; Numbers 13:25; Deuteronomy 9; 1 Kings 19:8; Jonah 3:4; Matthew 4:2 and parallels; Acts 1:3.

3The lectionary Gospel readings for the first two Sundays of Advent bring this message clearly upon us: Matthew 24:36-44 and Matthew 3:1-12; Mark 13:24-37 and Mark 1:1-8; Luke 21:25-36 and Luke 3:1-6.

4Laurence Hull Stookey, "Advent," in *The United Methodist Hymnal* (Nashville: The United Methodist Publishing House, 1989), p. 201. Alt. © 1989 The United Methodist Publishing House. Reprinted from *The United Methodist Hymnal* with permission.

5Darkness and light are another dominant biblical metaphor with applications for the seasons of Advent, Christmas, and Epiphany. We will not consider that set of images here, but further reading on the subject is encouraged (see especially Matthew 4:12-17; John 1:1-9).

6The Garden of Eden's fruit (Genesis 1:29-30), Nathan's ewe lamb parable (2 Samuel 12), Isaiah's wine and milk without price (Isaiah 55:1), the deer thirsting for water (Psalm 42:1), the prodigal's coveting of the swines' pods and the subsequent feast prepared on his behalf (Luke 15:11ff), and the great banquet (Matthew 22:1-14) are but a few examples of that biblical spread.

7Isaac Watts, "Joy to the World," *The United Methodist Hymnal* (Nashville: The United Methodist Publishing House, 1989), p. 246. Reprinted from *The United Methodist Hymnal* with permission.

[8]Alberto Taule, "Toda la Tierra," trans. Gertrude C. Suppe, *The United Methodist Hymnal* (Nashville: The United Methodist Publishing House, 1989), p. 210. English translation © 1989, The United Methodist Publishing House. Reprinted from *The United Methodist Hymnal* with permission.

[9]Eleanor Farjeon, "People, Look East," *The United Methodist Hymnal* (Nashville: The United Methodist Publishing House), p. 202. Used with permission.

Chapter 3

[1]T. S. Eliot, "Gerontion," *The Complete Poems and Plays* (New York: Harcourt, Brace and Company, Inc.,1952), p. 21. Used with permission.

[2]Isaac Watts, "Joy to the World," *The United Methodist Hymnal* (Nashville: The United Methodist Publishing House, 1989), p. 246. Reprinted from *The United Methodist Hymnal* with permission.

[3]Paraphrased from Howard Thurman, *The Mood of Christmas* (New York: Harper and Row, 1973), p. 23. © 1973 Howard Thurman. Used with permission.

[4]"The Great Thanksgiving for Christmas Eve, Day, or Season," *The United Methodist Book of Worship* (Nashville: The United Methodist Publishing House, 1992), p. 57. © 1992 The United Methodist Publishing House. Used with permission.

[5]Watts, *The United Methodist Hymnal*, p. 246. Reprinted from *The United Methodist Hymnal* with permission.

[6]Jaroslav J. Vajda, "Now the Silence," *The United Methodist Hymnal* (Nashville: The United Methodist Publishing House, 1989), p. 619. Words copyright © 1969 by Hope Publishing Co., Carol Stream, IL 60188. All rights reserved. Used with permission.

[7]Omer Westendorf, "You Satisfy the Hungry Heart," *The United Methodist Hymnal* (Nashville: The United Methodist Publishing House, 1989), p. 629. © Copyright permission obtained, Archdiocese of Philadelphia, 1977. All rights reserved.

[8]*We Gather Together; Services of Public Worship* (Nashville: The United Methodist Publishing House, 1972, 1976, 1979, 1980), p. 11. Used with permission.

Chapter 4

[1]T. S. Eliot, "Ash Wednesday," *The Complete Poems and Plays* (New York: Harcourt, Brace and Company, 1952), p. 66. Used with permission.

[2]"A Service of Ashes for Ash Wednesday," *The United Methodist Book of Worship* (Nashville: The United Methodist Publishing House, 1992), p. 323. © 1992 The United Methodist Publishing House. Used with permission.

[3]Cesareo Gabarain, "Una Espiga," trans. George Lockwood, *The United Methodist Hymnal* (Nashville: The United Methodist Publishing House, 1989), p. 637. English translation © 1989 The United Methodist Publishing House. Reprinted with permission.

[4]"A Service of Word and Table II," *The United Methodist Hymnal* (Nashville: The United Methodist Publishing House, 1989), p. 14. © 1972, 1985, 1989 The United Methodist House. Reprinted with permission.

[5]Joe Wise, "Take Our Bread," The United Methodist Hymnal (Nashville: The United Methodist Publishing House, 1989), p. 640. © 1966 by GIA Publications, Inc., Chicago, IL. All rights reserved. Used with permission.

Chapter 5

[1]Mark Searle, "Serving the Lord with Justice," *Liturgy and Social Justice*, eds. J. Frank Henderson, Kathleen Quinn, and Stephen Larson (Collegeville, MN: The Liturgical Press, 1980), p. 27. Reprinted by permission. All rights reserved.

[2]Brian Wren, "There's a Spirit in the Air," *The United Methodist Hymnal* (Nashville: The United Methodist Publishing House, 1989), p. 192. Words: Brian Wren © 1972 by Hope Publishing Co., Carol Stream, IL 60188. All rights reserved. Used with permission.

[3]By contrast, we can recall one of the images with which we began the study of Advent — hunger and the world's yearning for God's Messiah (see Chapter 3).

[4]Brian Wren, "Christ Is Risen," *The United Methodist Hymnal* (Nashville: The United Methodist Publishing House, 1989), p. 307. Words: Brian Wren © 1986 by Hope Publishing Co., Carol Stream, IL 60188. All rights reserved. Used with permission.

[5]Marion Hatchett, *Commentary on the American Prayer Book* (San Francisco: Seabury Press, 1981), pp. 383ff. © 1981 Harper Collins Publishers. Used with permission.

Chapter 6

[1]Friedrich Nietzsche, *Beyond Good and Evil* (New York: The Macmillan Company, 1923), p. 107. Used with permission.

[2]"A Service of Word and Table II," *The United Methodist Hymnal* (Nashville: The United Methodist Publishing House, 1989), p. 14. © 1972, 1985, 1989 The United Methodist Publishing House. Reprinted from *The United Methodist Hymnal* with permission.

[3]Ibid., p. 14. Reprinted from *The United Methodist Hymnal* with permission.

[4]Martin Luther, cited in *Context*, 18, no. 10 (May 15, 1986), p. 4; published by Claretian Publications. Reprinted with permission.

PART 2

Introduction

[1]"Preface," *The United Methodist Book of Worship* (Nashville: The United Methodist Publishing House, 1992), p. 3. Used by permission.

[2]Andy Langford, *Blueprints for Worship: A User's Guide for United Methodist Congregations* (Nashville: Abingdon Press, 1993). © 1993 by Abingdon Press. Used with permission.

[3]Michael E. Williams, *Preaching Pilgrims* (Nashville: Discipleship Resources, 1988), pp. 13-22.

Chapter 9

[1]For a good treatment of this subject, along with instructions for arranging and carrying out such a ministry, see Laurence Hull Stookey's text, *Eucharist: Christ's Feast with the Church*, Chapter 7 and Appendix 1.